Harry N. Abrams Inc., Publishers, New York

Carola Giedion-Welcker **Jean Arp** *Documentation Marguerite Hagenbach*

Milton S. Fox · Editor

Jean Arp and Hans Arp are identical, Mr. Arp using
both first names according to the language employed.

Translation by Norbert Guterman

Origin and Orientation

The works of Jean Arp are strange artistic growths, which spring from an ancient and richly stratified cultural soil. He was born in Strassburg, one of the most beautiful medieval cities of Europe. Its enchanting natural surroundings (the Vosges and the Black Forest are nearby) are matched by the medieval masterpieces within its walls, in a cathedral whose portals, sculptures, and mysterious space took several centuries to complete, and many other monuments in stone dating from all periods. Thus Arp from his earliest years had an abundant visual experience of art. At the same time he found in German romantic poetry visions of the past, the world of legend, the dreamlands of nature, and the marvelous domains of playful humor. As a boy he read Brentano's *Rheinmärchen*, fairy tales interwoven with impressions of a river voyage in a landscape populated with mythical figures, introducing him into fantastic realms. Later he was led deeper into these realms by the folksongs of *Des Knaben Wunderhorn*, and by Novalis' meditative, nature-inspired poetry. Through Mörike's *Wispeliaden*, dealing with the barber Wispel's whimsical jokes and puns, and written in a refreshingly spontaneous language, he became familiar with the magic of words. All these works are characterized by a free and witty expressiveness and imagination. Jean Arp, the future Dadaist, may even then have taken pleasure in buffoonish distortion and transformation of current linguistic usage. A world in which wonders and farce sprouted from one and the same root beckoned to him from every side.

Bibl. No. 42

v

Woodcut

At the same time, however, the future painter-poet from the Franco-German borderland became absorbed in the fiery world of Rimbaud. This French poet, whose mystical and sensual language achieves extraordinary suggestive force, explores hitherto inaccessible realms of the imagination. Through him a new poetic territory was disclosed to Arp, a psychic reality beyond the phenomenal world, in which life was created out of the basic elements of the word.

The circumstance that the scene of these first youthful impressions was a region that politically, culturally, and linguistically is both German and French was not without influence in his later development as an artist and poet. His German and French poems and his pictorial style reflect specific elements of both cultures. The union in his work of romantic fantasy with almost classical severity of proportions and clarity was doubtless furthered by the fact that he lived in a dual world. We have here a fusion of seemingly polar opposites, which incidentally makes itself felt also in many of his contemporaries, painters and poets.

He developed special bonds with Switzerland, too, where he went at an early age and later visited time and again. The several years he spent at Weggis with his family seemed to the maturing artist, who at that time felt the need for more extensive contacts with European cultural developments, an artificial idyll, almost like confinement. For this reason, the artistic "adventures" of this Weggis period are accounted for less by outside impulses than by his inner spiritual strivings. The "abstractions" he painted at that time caused his Swiss colleagues to shake their heads, but aroused the admiration of his friend Rossiné, the Russian painter. They were his first experiments in a quest for a new language of form (1909). We cannot help thinking of the solitary essays by the hero of Gottfried Keller's *Der grüne Heinrich*, whose linear cobweb fantasies were cut short when a "sensible" friend destroyed them as foolish aberrations. It is also noteworthy that Arp at that time experienced the Rigi landscape quite "abstractly," recording his impressions in graphic structures which "covered entire canvases and which were interwoven with strange scripts, runes, lines, and spots." They were, as he later wrote, "the result of months of tormenting labor." But this period of his development prepared him for the encounters and impressions of the following years, during which he exhibited at Herwarth Walden's gallery *Der Sturm* in Berlin and joined the *Blaue Reiter* in Munich, translating the stimulations he received trough Kandinsky into his own idiom. But it was only with his active participation in the intellectual and artistic battle that was fought by an international group of poets and painters in Zurich in the midst of the First World War (1916–1918) that his art began to unfold along entirely original lines.

Dadaland in Zurich

Zurich was the first center of the new movement, because this neutral island had become a meeting place of a generation of Europeans, who after a period of considerable material prosperity had been driven into the criminal disaster of a world war. It was clear-sighted youth that anticipated the defeat of the idea of rule by force, and at an early date recognized the demonic effects of the power neurosis and the divorce between technical ingenuity and wisdom. Arp felt spiritually akin to these "outsiders," who were actually the best representatives of their epoch. These poets, *diseuses*, *conférenciers*, painters, dancers, and architects were in rebellion against the prevailing moral standards and the "official" taste; at the same time they derided and parodied their own complicated and pointless everyday life, while the bloated nationalism that surrounded them only led to crises and wars. But they did not confine themselves to the game of *épater le bourgeois*, which was their version of the romantic struggle against Philistinism; these knights-errant of nonsense were also constructive, and strove for a new art and a new life, spiritualized and simplified. They radically repudiated "universal progress"; according to them, culture was to be found among the so-called barbarian primitives, and there was real barbarism in our over-organized, bureaucratic and mechanized civilization. They summoned the elementary force of "thought sprung from fantasy" in opposition to a view of the world originating in so-called common sense, and satirized the latter in poetic and pictorial manifestations. The growing opposition between the ideas of Vico and of Descartes, which is so topical today, was intuitively sensed even then. For what was the Dada movement but a revolt against a rationalistic universal system that had become untenable, against the superficial ideal of beauty on the classical model, against moral hypocrisy? "We must destroy, so that the lousy materialists may recognize in the ruins what is essential," Jean Arp wrote in retrospect, and to these words that sound like a manifesto he added that in his view the purpose of Dada was "to destroy the swindle of reason perpetrated on man in order to restore him to his humble place in nature."[1] Thus, behind the allegedly nihilistic

Dadaist attitudes lay a profound belief in long-forgotten beauty and humanity. The authentic *vox humana*, as Hugo Ball called it, was to make itself heard again, and come out against stifling materialism and intellectualization.

The artists who gathered in Zurich to form the *Cabaret Voltaire* (1916–1918) represented a cross section of European youth: Tristan Tzara and Marcel Janco came from Rumania; Hugo Ball, Emmy Hennings, and Richard Huelsenbeck from Germany; Otto and Mme. van Rees from Holland; Arp from Alsace and Paris; only Sophie Taeuber was a native of Zurich. All of them were anxiously seeking "the true, buried face of their time, its basic, essential features, the cause of its affliction and the possibility of its awakening." Art should be only "an occasion, a method" toward such an end, Hugo Ball says in *Die Flucht aus der Zeit* ("Escape from Time").[2] The Muse had come down from her pedestal; art was the expression of a profound spiritual vision, flowing from the unconscious life, and works of art could be created out of the humblest materials. In any event, there was no room here for the cult of genius. The Dadaists, for all their apparent absurdities, for all the deliberate shabbiness that characterized their artistic and literary output, had a clear and honest insight into the nature of their movement. According to Hugo Ball, Dada was "a fool's play originating in nothing, but in which all higher problems were involved."[3] Spontaneous imagination launched an offensive, at once gay and serious, against stale routine and artificial virtuosity.

Such were the guiding ideas of the Dadaists and of their *Cabaret Voltaire,* situated in the narrow Gothic Spiegelgasse of the old quarter in Zurich; they were also the ideas of the young Arp throughout his extremely active Zurich period. His works – reliefs, woodcuts, collages, tapestries, masks, and stage décors – bear the stamp of their time, but they also disclose a quest for primordial simplicity, for the essential, as well as an urge toward artistic anonymity. "Works of art should remain as anonymous in the great workshop of nature as are the clouds, the mountains, the seas, the animals, and man himself. Yes! Man should once again become part of nature, and artists should work collectively, as did the medieval artists." Thus Arp spoke, reflecting the atmosphere of those years. He himself seemed in those days something between a late-medieval "fool of God" and a modern dandy. His art, his thinking, his very being emanated relaxation, spontaneous wit, and charm. Hence his radical rejection of the hectic emotional pathos and theatricalism of the German Expressionists (although their participation in contemporary expression was evident) emerged from the spirit of the time, and marked a definitive repudiation of all pseudo-artistic attitudes, which had been officially cultivated in the preceding Wilhelmian era, and which now were criticized and ridiculed. The young Klee, too, had desperately resorted to satire in his early graphic works in order to launch an attack on his period and society, and in doing this he preferred a grim and grotesque style to that of sugar-coated *bellezza*. The young Italian Futurists had similarly discarded their Italian *bellezza* in favor of an expressive *anti-grazioso*.

IX

Abstract Composition – 1915 – Collage (paper, cardboard, and fabric) – 9³/₁₆ × 7⁷/₈″

Rectangles Arranged According to the Laws of Chance – 1916 – Collage (paper) – 10¹/₄ × 4¹⁵/₁₆″

X

XI   *Duo-Drawing Sophie and Jean Arp, torn and re-arranged – 1947 – Collage (paper and watercolor) – 11³/₄×9¹/₈"*

Constellation – 1955 – Collage (paper) – 11$^{15}/_{16}$×9$^{9}/_{16}$"

New Expressive Domains. The Everyday and the Infinite

Arp's reliefs, woodcuts, and collages thrived in this Zurich Dadaland, in a soil fertilized and stimulated by the most various cultural influences. There, too, his roguish poetry was first heard, in a language that sent up words like rockets. But to the Zurich public, and during the turbulent disputes within the Dada group, these facetious poems were also relaxing lyrical oases. As his friend Otto Flake said, "they thrust aside all psychological problems, and inaugurated a fantastic game, eliminating causality, and boldly skipping all intermediate links."[4] In this animated verbal world of "silver balls and fountains," of winged words and sonorous images, simultaneity was the trump card. The domains of the visible and the audible witnessed the birth of quite unusual things – strange symbioses and symbols, alluding equally to thoughts and things. The banal instruments of everyday life, which constitute our small world, now emerged as fragments, detached from their practical contexts to form other, purely pictorial or linguistic associations,[5] in a new existence (fig. 7, 10, 20). Elements of sound, rhythm, and proportion were dominant in Arp's pictorial and poetic works (fig. 1, 2, 3, 6, 7). A concise sign language, developed from forms and words, served to construct a detached, hovering universe, in which nothing was defined logically, but in which irrational zones open up with great suggestive force. Both the pictorial works and the poems repeatedly disclose the tragi-comic conflict between human smallness and cosmic infinity – a conflict to which our poor world is constantly exposed. Hence the dimensional contrasts in Arp, which draw their expressive force from both intellectual and formal elements. Peculiar formal entities arise – one might call them *Formlinge* (Frobenius' term for archetypal form-beginnings). Here, too, primeval shapes seem to come to life again and to act out a burlesque of today. For instance, a lone umbilical form floats like a tiny island in the cosmos of an enormously large page,[6] as did once the legendary island of Calypso in the mysterious center of the sea. Or a gigantic black *Arrow Cloud* threatens dot-like white entities that swirl around it (fig. 25). But the fact that from this new pictorial world *Constellations* and *Configurations* arise is the most important. For Arp is less interested in the fixed individual case than in the animated play of relationships, the sounds and echoes within that dynamic order in which everything fluctuates and is eternally subject to change and transformation (fig. 13, 17, 18, 20, 21, 23, 25, 27, 39, 42, 43, 48, 49, 98–101).

The Inner World Seeks Adequate Expression

In addition to this profoundly meaningful buffoonery or drollery, related in spirit to the marginal decorations of medieval Bibles and permeating the morality plays of those times, Jean Arp now developed another aspect of his being. It was an intensive listening to the central stillness of the inner world. His growing interest in Laotse's philosophy and Jakob Boehme's mystical writings points in the same direction. In his diary Arp speaks of "the infernal phantom of earthly confusion, disorder, futility and stupidity," against which one should "proceed with beating drums in order to make apparent the inconceivable madness of human activities"; and he adds in a distinctly religious vein: "We were attracted by the radiant brilliance of the mystical poems in which man is released from joys and sorrows. This was the 'carefree' ground of being, as the mystic Tauler called it." To the overactive busyness, the senseless turmoil of his epoch, the young Arp thus opposed inwardness, eternity. He recorded this inner absorption and spiritual asceticism, this turning away from the glitter of outward phenomena, in severe constructions composed of pure elements of form and color. Problems of content and of form merged; the early Zurich *Collages* (1915–1916) are actually pictorial meditations, expressions of that absorption. They are geometric compositions (fig. X), almost solemnly constructed, made of silver-gray or black-and-white papers, or held to Franciscan tones of gold, brown, and white. Everything is cut by machines in order to eliminate the human hand, which had been wielding "the brush stroke of genius" with such painful virtuosity. In their architectonic clarity and rhythmicality, these works have points of contact with Mondrian's creations, which Arp at that time had not seen. It should also be noted that, unlike Kandinsky, Arp did not call his works "compositions," but "architectural formations": "Our works are constructions of lines, surfaces, forms, colors. They attempt to approach reality. They hate artifice, vanity, imitation, tight-rope walking ... Art should lead to spirituality, to a mystical reality."[7]

Bibl. No. 46a

With this credo Arp defined the course he was to follow, and pointed to the deeper regions where he was later to anchor ever more resolutely. These *Collages,* with their austerity and ascetic rectangular design, were in striking contrast to the fluid, organic forms of his contemporary "objects reliefs," spontaneous creations full of witty associations, which were ordered according to "the laws of chance."[8] Just as "elementary" as the collages, the reliefs are above all characterized by their softly undulating organic forms and a burlesque quality, which we also find in many of his poems at that time, abounding in humorous attitudes, concentrated expressions, linguistic deformations, and grotesque verbal images. Their source is banal everyday life, but the words in the poems, just as the forms in the pictures, acquire rich new meanings. Here, too, for all the facetiousness, the way led through nonsense to that mysterious primal sense that slumbers deep below the world of phenomena and that can be approached – whether linguistically or pictorially – only in symbols that have many significations. Richard Huelsenbeck, whom Arp met in the Dada period and who has remained his friend to this day, regarded Arp's role as an artist within the modern movement as crucial. He wrote in the heyday of Dada: "Hans Arp's art is the first that – since the Cubist transvaluation – has discovered a dogma to resolve all difficulties, spasms, and convulsions . . . A new will to spirituality has appeared."[9]

The two essential features of the entirely new method of artistic creation that Arp conceived at that time – organic form flowing from the depths of the irrational and abstract articulation by means of elementary geometric figures – implied rejection of the predominance of the material world, and of an artistic expression by the means of a virtuoso-like illusionism. In both respects the new art asserted the *inner image*, which was to be grasped by unprecedented methods, deliberately simple and austere – *les moyens pauvres*, as Stravinsky called them referring to the domain of music. This double orientation toward organic form and abstract articulation – we might also speak of an intimate interweaving of classical and romantic "climates" – was to define the basic directions of modern art. Arp as early as 1916 anticipated developments to come.

"Word and Image Are One" (Hugo Ball, 1916)

Like Klee, the painter-poet Arp used captions for his visual creations to add a voice from another realm and to do away with the rigid demarcation line separating the word from the image, and at the same time to point a way to their interpenetration. Indeed, the very fact of his own parallel activities contributed to the merging of the normally separate domains of art. Merely by reading the poetic titles of Arp's works in chronological order, we can follow his artistic path and his successive changes of emphasis. At first he is concerned with paradoxical and unusual configurations, with oppositions and connections between symbols of human and of inanimate things. The captions always refer to "magic fragments," to bizarre formations that are detached from their usual contexts, splinters of a great all-pervading being and becoming, which are brought into new, unusual relationships and strange new combinations. His *Eye and Navel Dress* (fig. 12) stretches triangularly, bends into a double arc, and is in fact the pictorial version of his lyrical *Pyramidal Petticoat*. Curved mustaches, floating neckties, and fluttering lips seem to perform their undulating movements on a cosmic scale, as if they were great elemental forces. Swooping umbilical forms, masks of men and of birds leer at us, church clocks beat time with oval pestles (fig. 4–6, 12, 13).[10] The specific form here is not the straight, but the organic, wavy line. Everything is vibrating in a world where man, closely interwoven with the cosmos and with things, has lost his uniqueness and exists only as an absurd fragment. Along with all else, man is drawn into eternal change, like natural forms, and like the latter, is animated by the all-comprehensive "universal spirit" of the romantics. The long-buried primeval pattern of the human seems to re-emerge, as though out of a deep recollection, as a torso or vase form (fig. 7–9, XXV, XXVI).

Arp restores essential mythical existence to man and things. That is why man, in his works, is not a rational being enthroned above all else, but himself an element of nature, a thing, a part of one great fate, a solitary leaf adrift in the space of worlds and times. Therewith a bridge is thrown out leading from inwardness to mythical forms. All around us there is an all-comprehensive net of relationships involving things large and small, important and unimportant (fig. 18, 25, 38, 46–49), and a bubbling fantasy and irony are at work perpetually destroying the bombastic illusion of man's supremacy. Man is identified with things, while things are identified with man. New spiritual and formal proportions have made their appearance, and a new world of unity and interrelatedness arises from disunion and separateness.

The same message resounds in his poetry of those years, speaks out of the folds of his *Pyramidal Petticoat*,[11] is trumpeted from the housing of his *Cloud Pump*, and chirps in his *Triparted Bird* (fig. XVIII, XX). It is as though the poet were shaking up a large bag full of famous sayings, everyday words, and prefabricated clichés, in order to make us aware of them out of context. Everything that has until now been ordered according to a rigid hierarchy of values, enters into new relationships governed by the free laws of imagination and association. In his linguistic, just as in his visual creations, Arp here goes back to the elements in sound and form. He disregards continuous narrative, just as in his pictures he disregards rational perspective. In his pictures and his poems a simultaneous and richly stratified life prevails – a great flowing from sound to sound, from form to form, which is nevertheless rigidly held together and constitutes a compositional whole. Since his Dada period in Zurich, and even earlier, from his participation in the *Blaue Reiter* movement in Munich, Arp has been *both* a poet and a plastic artist, producing imaginative and disciplined poems, graphic works, and reliefs. We are reminded of Kandinsky, who said that each time he switched from poetry to painting or vice versa, he "merely changed instruments." No Dada publication appeared without Arp's many-sided contributions in the form of humorous verse, woodcuts, and cover designs (fig. XIII, XV). His visual creations are sometimes fluid and mobile, and sometimes symmetrically articulated with architectonic severity. These two orientations – toward the natural and toward the urban – were even then expressed very intensively. His burlesque poems are illustrated by his rhythmic black and white forms, and words and forms have equal force. Never is his poetic creation a mere accompaniment to his pictorial work; the life of the former is always as full, as rich, and as joyous as that of the latter. Throughout that period Arp's compositions are often like kinds of written images that emerge from the depths of a fantastic world (fig. XVIII–XX), constructed with lines and planes, or moving seismically to the pulsations of an inner rhythm. Arp spontaneously rediscovers Novalis' "marvelous and secret code of nature" and embodies it in a modern artistic form. This is often suggested by his captions, such as *Objets placés comme écriture* ("Objects Arranged as Writing"), and many similar ones (fig. 14, 16). Such an intimate relationship with written characters can often be detected in modern art, for instance in the symbolic or formally expressive part played by letters and words in Cubist pictures, or in Paul Klee, who developed a hieroglyphic language, and invented a pictorial "plant script," "picture script," and "abstract script", while Arp composed "string reliefs" (fig. 14–17) in "written" forms and rhythms.

If only because of his dual talents, Arp has always been inclined to place the word in a pictorial setting, and to decorate books, the vehicles of the word. Even after the Zurich period, during his Surrealist years in Paris, and down to the present, he has always invented fantastic, yet amazingly simple pictorial accompaniments to his own and his friends' poetic texts. In Zurich, Arp provided the manifestoes and poems of the Dadaists with vignettes and full-page illuminations. Large-scale individual forms and interwoven groups of forms here carry on their roguish play, or are articulated as solemn black-and-white rhythms, serving as visual support to the text. This, for instance, is the case with Richard Huelsenbeck's *Phantastische Gebete* ("Fantastic Prayers," 1916), in which the author's drum-beating language is matched by Arp's sonorous "chords" – abstract, often severely symmetrical compositions. The veins of the wood on which they are engraved lend them an irregular natural quality, and at the same time make us constantly aware of the presence of the material which helped to shape them. In Tristan Tzara's *Cinéma calendrier du coeur abstrait* ("Film Calendar of the Abstract Heart") of 1920 (fig. XIX) entire pages are covered with irrationally flowing dreamy forms, which spread out like a moving

Bibl. No. 2

black web – these are no doubt maturer versions of his early attempts at Weggis. The passive, unconscious following of the inner flux, which the Surrealists later named *automatisme psychique,* is here kept in control and balanced by a perpetually alert sensibility. The cover for the periodical *Der Zeltweg* (fig. XV) is an outstanding example of monumental clarity and nobility in its sure arrangement of planes, forms, and letters, where playful jagged lines are fused with softly flowing ones into a tightly-knit unity.

Stimulations and Original Paths

In tracing the sources of Arp's idiom, we may assume that his early graphic works were to some extent influenced by Kandinsky who, in 1912, in his book *Über das Geistige in der Kunst* ("On the Spiritual in Art"), in his collection of lyrical poems *Klänge* ("Sonorities"), and in the *Blaue Reiter* yearbook presented modern graphic works of an entirely new character. Arp, who contributed to that yearbook, was stimulated by Kandinsky's engravings to develop his own method of graphic "illumination" on an identical non-illustrative basis. In retrospect we recognize that Arp anticipated many things that were to be realized on a large scale, in book production and advertising, only in the course of the following decades. His drawings in the periodicals, books and manifestoes, which were then printed in limited editions by W. Heuberger in Zurich, and which today are collector's items, are characterized by breadth of treatment, and sure typographic instinct in harmonizing text and pictures. This new plastic language expressed a profoundly original vitality. Whereas Kandinsky's wood engravings suggest an explosive, flaming handwriting, Arp's signs flow smoothly despite their firm structure. Significantly, he himself at that period called these works "pictorial constructions." Moreover, Arp's quieter, lyrical tone stands out clearly from the dramatic passion of Kandinsky's early creations.

The intensive interplay of forms, and of forms and surfaces, has remained a constant feature of Arp's works and is present in his reliefs as well as in his sculptures in the round. He achieves a mysterious correspondence between external and internal movement, between active structuring and elastic yielding, and between black and white tones. The combination of the organic and the constructive, the "vegetative" and "planned" principles, which pervades his entire *oeuvre,* was present even then, and to this day it has been the hallmark of his art. We rediscover it in his *Geometric-Ageometric* sculptures and reliefs, which he assigns to an "intermediate realm," and many of which he entitles *Interregnum*, no doubt suggesting that here the most various languages of form interpenetrate (fig. 40, 41, 75, 78–81).

His conception of the pedestal also makes use of both expressive potentialities. In his early period Arp provides no base for his sculptures, which are as though lost in nature, or he gives them organically undulating bases, which grasp the sculptural parts and hold them together, as might also happen in nature (fig. 48, 49, 52, 53, 64, 65 top). This method is consistent with his idea that art should be anonymous and integrated with nature as a whole. On the other hand, we see that his treatment of the base, particularly in his later works, is carried out in an architectonic language: the base becomes a terminal point, a boundary, or a mediating element between the sculpture and the constructed environment (fig. 68, 70, 71, 76, 77, 92, 93). The treatment of the base has today become an extraordinarily difficult and important problem in the presentation of a sculpture,[12] and the base is to an increasing extent conceived of as a peripheral component of the work itself. Arp has often used parts of earlier sculptures as bases for new ones; in their new subordinate function they appear with completely changed proportional and tensional contrasts (fig. 59, 82, 84).

Bibl. No. 3

Bibl. No. 54

Elementary Pictorial Forms

The general "elementarism" and the clear mathematical structure of Arp's compositions enabled him (as well as Miro) to keep aloof from literary description even during the years of his active participation in the Surrealist movement (1924–1928) in Paris, and assert the primary pictorial relationships, while his subject matter continued

Bibl. No. 61

to suggest recollection and mythical elements. Accordingly the response to his art was dual, too, and he gained recognition in opposing camps. Piet Mondrian, the Dutch painter who was imbued with mathematical discipline, saw in Arp's creations "neutral, completely indeterminate forms against a neutral background";[13] in a broader sense, he considered Arp's method a variation and confirmation of his own purely geometric and universal "neo-plastic" paintings, which eliminated every suggestion of figurative representation, and in which the character of the picture was decided only by the austere counterpoising of pure colors in balanced relationships. This was "the new culture of pure relations," as Mondrian put it. On the other hand, Max Ernst reacted positively and affirmatively to the elements of content in Arp's work: he underlined Arp's "hypnotic language which takes us back to a lost paradise, to cosmic secrets, and teaches us to understand the language spoken by the universe." Arp's creations conjure up the most mysterious depths of nature, as Novalis had experienced them.[14]

Bibl. No. 61

After his Dada years, the poet Hugo Ball turned toward religion, and found a deepened inner culture, opposed to the superficial civilization of progress, in the Christian-romantic spirit of Novalis. Arp, who in 1926 had moved to Meudon near Paris, after joining the newly rising Surrealist movement, gradually turned from his early burlesque interpretations of life to the fusion of natural and human substance into a new sculptural unity. He produced anonymous forms, symbols of life, in which the tragic rifts, dividing the human, the natural, and the artificial were bridged. They were objectivized and self-contained entities whose universal and elementary forms logically continued the earlier reliefs. The title *Concrétion humaine*, which emerges at the beginning of the series, and is often repeated later, evokes the comprehensive natural process of condensation, of dynamic convergence: "Concretion is the result of a process of crystallization: the earth and the stars, the matter of the stone, the plant, the animal, man, all exemplify such a process. Concretion is something that has grown."[15]

While in his early period he expressed the tension between man and the world through the shock of unusual forms and proportions – an approach that both in form and content often survives in the grotesque designs of his sculptures (fig. 54–60) – he now formulates the mysterious life and fusion of nature and man with ever greater vigor and breadth in a daring and joyful plastic language (fig. 51–53, 64, 69).

"Art is a fruit that grows in man, like a fruit on a plant, or a child in its mother's womb. But whereas the fruits of the plant, of the animal, of the mother's womb assume autonomous and natural forms, art, the spiritual fruit of man, usually resorts to forms that are ridiculously like other things. Only in our time has plastic art freed itself from reproducing mandolins, presidents in cutaway suits, battles or landscapes. I love nature, but not its substitutes. Naturalistic, illusionist art is a substitute."[16]

It is noteworthy that Arp came to sculpture in the round by way of reliefs. He began to make these in his early period, and even today he devotes part of his interest to them. We can follow him as he gradually detaches the relief from the wall, places it in free space, rounds it more and more, and in the end transforms the relief elements into fully rounded sculptural configurations, displaying again the most impressive form relationships (fig. 44–46). The elementary shapes and the intricate ralationships are as crucial here as they were in the reliefs. In 1935 he begins to produce sculptures that summarize and synthesize his previous experiments (fig. 50–53, 61, 64, 65, 82, 83). These monumental works, revealing a distinguished and sublimated sense for treatment of the expanded volumes, are found side by side with works that are playfully burlesque in their capricious formations. The humorous, bizarre goblin and elf play continues throughout all periods of his creation from 1917 on, producing fairytale beings, hybrid and magic (fig. 54–61), but his symbols of nature occupy a far greater place in his *oeuvre*. What is nature for Arp? An immense vital process, both extraordinarily simple and complex, a cycle evolving between birth and death, constantly changing and growing, and hence to be grasped only dynamically, never statically in the field of art (fig. 62, 63, 82, 83, 85, 92, 93).

Arp's genetic orientation, his untiring search for the "archetype," and his deep aspiration to penetrate into the innermost original shape and structure of creation are suggested also by his personal confessions and diary entries. He, too, was drawn to that original cause of all formative powers in nature, which for the painter Paul Klee was the home and starting point of authentic art. We can detect in Arp the same profound experience of life, which conceives of creation as an eternal process, as permanent transformation and growth, not as being, not as a ready-made product of nature. This is why Arp's initial forms strike us as being so ready to be transmuted, so filled with inner organic tension. Whereas Brancusi emphasizes an almost religious element of worship in his sculptures, and pursues the ideal of extracting purest form from matter – in a sense that is perhaps a modern revival of antiquity – Arp's sculptures, for all their arbitrariness, usually retain an anonymous quality: they are lost in space and in dream, and are directly connected with stones and trees. But in a certain respect, his art, like Brancusi's, is sometimes characterized by a Mediterranean self-sufficiency and harmony, which clarify and expose form in its splendor and beauty (fig. 66–71, 76, 77, 79). He creates well-balanced, joyful pieces alongside those others that mysteriously emerge from long-buried forests and fairylands. This fantastic world includes "stones that are as though formed by human hand" or stones that are "exposed" in the landscape like foundlings (fig. 48, 62), and he speaks of these stones as of fabulous beings, which are nevertheless intimately connected with him: "A dead stone suddenly opens its eyes, and sends out swarms of singing glances. Sometimes stones are like children. They babble on and on, and the sculptor is only too willing to believe what they are saying. To enlarge a stone is difficult work. Stones that cling to the sculptor are dangerous: they obstruct his path to God."[17]

Here once again Arp deliberately turns his back on so-called "creative genius" in favor of artistic anonymity, and thus comes close to the oriental conception of quietly radiating things – including those that have not been touched or changed by human hand, as they can be seen in Japanese gardens or markets where stones are sold like choice fruit. But this is also the language of a certain contemporary romantic spirit, which is not tied to the period or the hour, but seeks to penetrate to the authentic vital core of things. How close this poetic world of Arp's dreams and creations comes also to the sphere of natural science may be seen from the fact that the English biologist Waddington, according to whom growth and individuation of form are characteristic of organic life, uses Arp's sculptures as supplements to his scientific illustrations.[18]

Bibl. No. 20 →

Arp's sculpture in the round starts from the self-contained volume. But just as in his woodcuts he discloses an interplay of positive and negative forms, so in his sculptures, he often permeates his mass with light and air, and obtains striking effects by allowing air to circulate freely around the forms. Brancusi applies the same principle only in his wood sculptures, and Henry Moore occasionally achieves the same effect by "enshelling" his surfaces. Arp's *Snake Bread* (fig. 65), smooth, without joints, curls around a well-like hollow. The upward-striving *Garland of Buds* (1936, fig. 95) and *Star* (1939, fig. 94) spread out into space and are articulated by their encircling of it, while the significant *Ptolemy* (1953, fig. 96, 97) in its serpentine, homogeneously flowing circumscription of airy zones describes a circling in space, which suggests both in form and content the philosopher's system that was built around a cosmic center of the world. Here too Arp achieves in the transmutations or in the synthesis of the "vegetative" and "constructive" principles a sculptural form that, like his reliefs, can exist *within* and harmonizes *with* architecture (fig. 30). The fact that all his creations fit in easily with their environment – even though the forms are sometimes purely organic – is shown by the early murals in the Aubette nightclub at Strassburg (1927–1928). We can also understand why his gigantic and grotesque organisms, thanks to their elementary clarity and rhythm, disclosing essential proportional contrasts, can find their place in Theo van Doesburg's and Sophie Taeuber's geometric interior architecture and decoration (fig. 98, 99). His burlesque shapes – masks and mustached heads, torsos and giant-navels on a dark ground, or friezes of enormous mushroom caps running under the edge of the ceiling – do not seem to dissolve the severe architecture, but animate it with new natural rhythms. Surely those who had the good fortune to dance in this modern prehistoric cavern moved not merely to the sounds of jazz, but were also inspired by the visual vitality and rhythms of Arp's creations, which articulated the walls and the space, reaching out like monumental tentacles full of facetiousness and relaxation.[19]

The same is true of sculptures such as *Shepherd of Clouds* (1949–1953, fig. 61) with its abundant floating shapes. When it was temporarily exhibited in the square of the old town of Yverdon (in 1954), it fitted in easily with the old tower and the Baroque houses; now, in front of the library of the University of Caracas (Venezuela), its actual destination, this fantastic being placed among plants, architecture, and various structures is effective, independent and yet not isolated, in full harmony with this entirely different environment.

The wood reliefs that Arp created for the bar of the Graduate Center at Harvard (Cambridge) in 1950 seem less facetious than the Strassburg mural; yet they brighten the surroundings with a penetrating lyrical accent. Like passing stars, clouds, birds and leaves, the forms move along the regularly veined wooden wall, broadening finally into "constellations." It is relaxed poetic interplay of motions, forms and surfaces. Arp's fantastic world is here incorporated into the daily life of a young generation, which lives in this environment. Walter Gropius, by coupling with his building these irrational spheres that transcend its spatial and functional tasks, gave proof of an especially sensitive understanding of our present needs.

Bibl. No. 138

The most recent reliefs, at the University of Caracas, are precisely cut and roundly undulant forms which describe their movement before great wall surfaces in a script-like manner. The hovering interplay of open and closed forms, perforated and continuous surfaces, is executed in the language of a fantastic geometry, which reminds one of Oriental calligraphy or shadow puppets. Arp seems to come ever closer to those domains. Already his india-ink drawings, the black cadences accompanying Richard Huelsenbeck's *New York Cantata* (1952), came close to a monumental pictorial language (fig. XXXI, XXXII). But even apart from the works directly connected with and planned for architecture, Arp's graphic productions seem predestined for interiors and walls, adding a human note and at the same time rhythmic accents harmonizing with the architectural whole. His magnificently soaring simple forms are just as much at home in a wood-panelled peasant house as in a modern city bar or café.[20]

XXXI

"Art Should Lead to Spirituality, to Reality – to Mystical Reality" (Jean Arp)

The basic aspiration of the art that for more than four decades has been called "modern" is perhaps to make an invisible reality visible – to discover a visual language capable of capturing the spiritual spheres beyond the world of phenomena. Such an inner vision has been embodied in various ways in the works of Kandinsky, Klee, Mondrian, Brancusi, and Pevsner, to name only a few. Arp, who took this path at an early date, has also been led to a completely new conception of matter. At first, matter was for him a primary element of tension, an autonomous conglomerate whose silent language the artist was to awaken pictorially. In the course of the years he has gradually shifted the emphasis onto the spiritual forces of man, in the feeling that only they have continuous existence. Now matter is subject to the artist's free choice, and is interesting only as a medium for expressing a higher reality. Arp regards this higher reality alone as indestructible and eternal, and everything material as inevitably fragile and transient. His *papiers déchirés* – "torn papers" (fig. XI) mark the introduction of the tragic element of transitoriness, of death, into his work: this element is anticipated, included in the composition in advance. This new attitude toward time, and the presence of death in life, was furthered in Arp by a personal tragedy – the sudden death (in 1943) of his wife, whose inner light and clarity contributed a quality of faith to his life and creative struggle. The clear and firmly structured *Collages* which he composed, partly in collaboration with her, in his early Zurich period (fig. IX, X) yielded to compositions of pieces of torn material, on which lies the shadow of transience. Thus the spiritual attitude flows from the *process* of work

Bibl. No. 138

itself. In this connection it may be interesting to quote a remark by which the Danish writer Alexander Partens qualified Arp's artistic methods: "It was the distinction of Jean Arp," he said, "to have at a certain moment discovered that the craft itself is a problem. He was no longer concerned with improving a given aesthetic system, he wanted direct production."[21] Thus the mode of production, the artistic form, and the spiritual attitude were woven into a higher unity.

Bibl. No. 100

Arp's later poems, some of which refer to Sophie Taeuber's death, also disclose a shift to profound meditation, to the elusively transparent qualities of the word, which stem from elegiac folksongs rather than from the artist's spontaneous fancy. All of them reflect a quest for the long-forgotten, buried primeval image of nature and man, a breakthrough to the original source of Being.

Arp in all his periods is spiritually akin to the German romantics: like them, he endows the created world with a soul, and seeks to establish an essential unity between man and nature. His ironic wit, which reflects a characteristic intellectual freedom and alertness, is also a feature of German romanticism. The fact that along with daring fantasies he creates almost classically pure structures, and that among his works we find joyful marble fruits, illumined by an inner sun (fig. 66, 70), side by side with nocturnal forms, enigmatic and dreamy (fig. 90, 91), may well be rooted in his Franco-Alemanic origin. In 1941–1942 his production was stimulated by the

Bibl. No. 100

serene beauty that surrounded him at Grasse where he enjoyed a last Arcadian idyll with his wife (fig. 32, 68–71). But the Mediterranean features of his art are not merely due to external influences, such as his stay at the French coast, or his trips to Greece, where he was deeply impressed by the prehistoric and archaic epochs of Hellenic sculpture. It was within himself that he bore those shapes of simple harmony, such as those primordial vase contours and torso forms that he transmuted into the idol-like image of man, or developed into torso-trees such as the *Daphne* (fig. 92, 93).

The motif of the torso-vase or humanized amphora emerges repeatedly from his earliest period on, and occupies a dominant place in his work, both in two- and three-dimensional treatments (fig. 7–9, 19, 86–89). Things and man are fused in simple and pure forms that are reminiscent of the Cycladic idols. Both Paul Klee and Oskar Schlemmer have in this sense brought the vase and man into unity, whereas the undulant body of the guitar, which continually appears in Picasso's work, reawakens only remote and formal – rather than mythical – associations with the primeval human type. But in Arp, after his long wanderings through the world of objects in his Dada period and the world of natural symbolism in the later periods, the slumbering archetype of the human seems to come back to life from the depths of memory (fig. 88, 89). As early as 1916, Hugo Ball had written prophetically: "If I understand him well, he is concerned less with richness than with simplification . . . To form, means for him to delimit himself against the indefinite and the nebulous. He strives to purify the imagination, and concentrates less on exploring its treasure of images than on discovering the basic pattern of these images."[22] These words remain true today. By freely adopting an austere expressive method, Arp has brought about a renascence of essential form in many domains of art. That is why his interest is repeatedly directed toward the early periods of art and thinking, and time and again he returns to the ideas of primitive Christianity and the pre-Socratic philosophy of nature, to that eternally changing cosmos of Heraclitus, and the *theos agenetos*, the most primitive divine being, which Thales of Miletus describes as "the still unborn God." And like those early ascetics, thinkers, and poets, Arp dreams (with burlesque undertones) cosmic dreams, connections and transmutations. Thus he writes:

"From a sailing cloud a leaf emerges to the surface. The leaf changes into a vase. An immense navel appears. It grows, it becomes larger and larger. The sailing cloud dissolves in it. The navel has become a sun, an immense source, the fountainhead of the world. It radiates. It has become light. It has become the essential."

Bibl. No. 78

Bibl. No. 4

NOTES

[1] Hans Arp, "Notes from a diary", *Transition*, No. 21, 1932.

[2] Hugo Ball, *Die Flucht aus der Zeit* ("Escape from Time"), Munich, Duncker & Humblot, 1927.

[3] Ibid.

[4] Otto Flake, *Nein und Ja*, Roman, Frankfurt, S. Fischer, 1920 (p. 76).

[5] Morgenstern, for all his grotesque absurdities, does retain narrative elements, while Arp develops his spiritual climate exclusively from the sound and the associative interplay of words.

[6] *7 Arpaden,* Hannover, Merz-Verlag, 1923.

[7] Jean Arp, *On My Way – Poetry and Essays, 1912-1947,* New York, Wittenborn, Schultz, Inc., 1948 (p. 82).

[8] The term "laws of chance" is appropriate here, because the rational human rules are eliminated to make room for fate whose laws follow a higher logic. Moreover, in this context "chance" does not stand for "chaos" (as H. Sedlmayr arbitrarily interprets it), but for "fortunate coincidence."

[9] "Die Arbeiten von Hans Arp," *Dada*, No. 3, Zurich, 1918.

[10] Cf. the linguistic parallels in "Second Hand" and "Arabian Hourglass," in the volume of poems *Der Pyramidenrock.* (The youthful impressions of the Strassburg cathedral clock with its fantastic play of rhythms seem often to echo in Arp's works.)

[11] In which the severe structure of the pyramid, the banal petticoat, and the romantic wonder bird "Rock" of the same name, are brought into surprising unison.

[12] Brancusi has always attached great importance to this problem.

[13] Piet Mondrian, *L'Art Nouveau et la Vie Nouvelle,* 1931. (English translation in: C. L. Jaffé, *De Stijl,* 1917-1931, Amsterdam, Meulenhoff, 1956.)

[14] Text by Max Ernst for the catalogue of the Arp exhibition "Art of This Century" gallery, New York, 1944.

[15] Hans Arp, *Unsern täglichen Traum* ("Our Daily Dream"), Zurich, Verlag der Arche, 1955 (p. 83).

[16] Hans Arp, "Notes from a diary", *Transition*, No. 21, 1932.

[17] Hans Arp, *Unsern täglichen Traum* ("Our Daily Dream"), Zurich, Verlag der Arche, 1955 (p. 102).

[18] *Aspects of Form in Nature and Art,* London, ed. L. Whyte, 1951.

[19] Unfortunately, these unique documents were replaced (painted over) with cheap naturalistic pictures. The related large-scale Miros in the country house of the architect Paul Nelson at Varangeville on the Channel coast (painted in 1938) were destroyed during the war.

[20] Monumental woodcuts of Arp in *Elemente* by Hans Arp, Zurich, ed. Karl Schmid, 1950.

[21] Alexander Partens, "Dadakunst", in *Dada Almanach,* ed. R. Huelsenbeck, Berlin, Erich Reiss, 1920 (p. 84).

[22] Hugo Ball, *Die Flucht aus der Zeit* ("Escape from Time"), Munich, Duncker & Humblot, 1927 (p. 80).

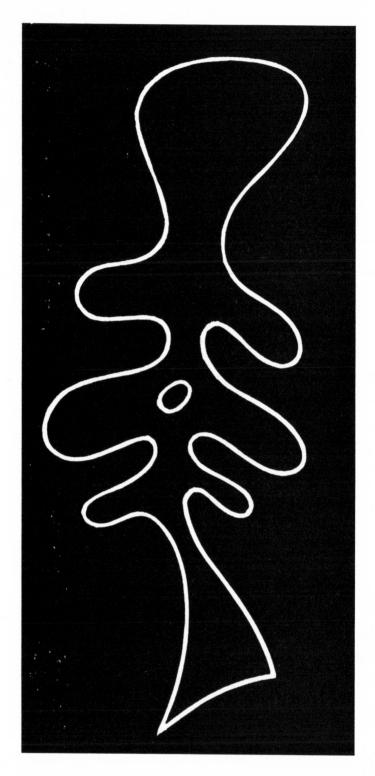

Bibl. No. 296

Kaspar is dead   *Bibl. No. 105*

alas our good kaspar is dead.

who will now carry the burning banner hidden in the pigtail of clouds to play the daily black joke.

who will now turn the coffee-mill in the primeval barrel.

who will now entice the idyllic deer out of the petrified paper box.

who will now confound on the high seas the ships by addressing them as parapluie and the winds by calling
      them keeper of the bees ozone spindle your highness.

alas alas alas our good kaspar is dead. holy ding dong kaspar is dead.

the cattlefish in the bellbarns clatter with heartrending grief when his christian name ist uttered. that is why I
      keep on moaning his family name kaspar kaspar kaspar.

why have you left us. into what shape has your beautiful great soul migrated. have you become a star or a
      watery chain attached to a hot whirlwind or an udder of black light or a transparent brick on the groaning
      drum of jagged being.

now the part in our hair the soles of our feet are parched and the fairies lie half-charred on the pyre.

now the black bowling alley thunders behind the sun and there's no one to wind up the compasses and the
      wheels of the handbarrows any more.

who will now eat with the phosphorescent rat at the lonely barefooted table.

who will now chase away the siroccoco devil when he wants to beguile the horses.

who will now explain to us the monograms in the stars.

his bust will adorn the mantelpieces of all truly noble men but that's no comfort that's snuff to a skull.

Weggis 1912.

(On My Way – Poetry and Essays 1912-1947. Wittenborn, Schultz, Inc., New York, 1948. Translated by Ralph Manheim. P. 10.)

XXXVII

Opus Zero

I am the great he-she-it
The strong and rigorous regiment
The ozone stalk quite prima Qua
Anonymous and one per cent.

The P. P. Tit. and also Po-
Posauna with mouth and hole
The giant herculean pot
The right cook with the lefthand foot.

I am the splendid long-life-long
The twelfth sense in the ovary
The perfect complete Augustine
Wrapt in a cellulosian frock.

(1915-1924)

Sekundenzeiger

dass ich als ich
ein und zwei ist
dass ich als ich
drei und vier ist

dass ich als ich
wieviel zeigt sie
dass ich als ich
tikt und takt sie

dass ich als ich
fünf und sechs ist
dass ich als ich
sieben acht ist

dass ich als ich
wenn sie steht sie
dass ich als ich
wenn sie geht sie

dass ich als ich
neun und zehn ist
dass ich als ich
elf und zwölf ist

(1915-1924)

l'étoile ternit
elle se mire sans se voir
elle est un mot fané
elle est un oeil sans regard

elle était une fleur
qui battait comme un coeur
elle était un coeur
qui fleurissait comme une fleur

la nuit s'écaille
elle fait naître la vie
le coq qui pleure
devient le coq qui rit

il hisse la flamme
du rêve et de l'amour
pour le cap de soie
pour le paysage du jour   (1941)

To Sophie

All flowers bloom
Bloom for You
All hearts glow
Glow for You

Now You are gone
Why should I stay
If it only could be
That You came back to me

All skies bloom
Bloom for You
All stars glow
Glow for You

(1943)

Bibl. No. 177

Bibl. No. 177

Clouds

The clouds are ghosts that haunt the drifting spaces.
With soft hands, soft arms, and exaggeratedly soft movements
They lead sweet-smelling moons to their mouths.
Pining away they consume the moons.
A man draws clouds on a sheet of paper
And fills the clouds with little crosses.
A bird settles silently in front of him
And gazes at him with bottomless eyes.
Silent birds are messengers of the dead.
They settle fearless before the man
And bring him in their bottomless eyes
Brightly shining sparks, greetings from the realm of the dead.
One cloud lies naked in the dark.
It sleeps and dreams.
One cloud lies naked in the dark.
It is beautiful like my beloved.

(1939-1945)

1887 Born in Strassburg, September 16.

At the age of fifteen he became attached to the work of the German Romantic Clemens Brentano and established contact with the "Stürmer" group to which, among others, the poets Flake, Schickele, and Stadler belonged.

1904 First stay in Paris with relatives and first visual contact with modern painting. Student at the School of Applied Arts in Strassburg. Sent a first collection of poems, *Logbuch,* to the Seemann Verlag, but the manuscript was lost. Three of his poems appeared in René Schickele's review, *Das Neue Magazin.*

1905 In his anthology of contemporary Alsacian poetry (Strassburg, 1905) Karl Gruber spoke of the young poet in these terms: "In the 'Stürmer' group we today find Hans Arp, aged eighteen. He regards himself as a pupil of Mombert and of Schur – influences probably due only to chance. In his *Logbuch* of 1904 there is still a good deal of stammering and spluttering instead of clear images; it is the book of a child, but of an exceptionally sensitive child full of great poetic receptivity. Where childlike imagination proceeds on its own and at the same time is able to use language, naïveté suddenly becomes beauty, a delicate kind of beauty, gently smiling, yet which, with its tapering fingers, has the power of plucking questions and vistas from unsuspected depths."

1905–1907 Pupil of Ludwig von Hofmann at the Weimar Art School. Visited the modern exhibitions of Count Harry von Kessler and the architect Henry van de Velde.

1908 Worked at the Académie Julian in Paris.

1909 In Weggis, Switzerland. Here he met the painters Gimmi, Helbig, Lüthy, and others, with whom, in 1911, he founded the "Moderne Bund."

1911 Co-organizer of the first exhibition of the "Moderne Bund" at the Hotel du Lac, Lucerne, with works by Amiet, Arp, Friesz, Gauguin, Gimmi, Helbig, Herbin, Hodler, Huber, Lüthy, Matisse, and Picasso. Paid a visit to Kandinsky, in Munich. Contact with the artists of the "Blaue Reiter."

1912 Participated in the second exhibition of the "Blaue Reiter" in Munich, and in the second exhibition of the "Moderne Bund," at the Kunsthaus in Zurich. Contributed to the book *Der Blaue Reiter*. Became acquainted with Delaunay.

1913 Contributed to the review *Der Sturm* (Herwarth Walden). Took part in the first "Herbstsalon" at the Sturm Gallery in Berlin. Co-editor with L. H. Neitzel of *Neue Französische Malerei* (Verlag der Weissen Blätter, Leipzig).

1914 Meetings with Max Ernst at the "Werkbund" exhibition, in Cologne.

1914 Paris. Became acquainted with Max Jacob, Modigliani, Viking Eggeling, Arthur Cravan. Made contact with Picasso through Max Jacob. Met Apollinaire at the Delaunays. Modigliani drew his portrait.

1915 Moved to Zurich in the course of the summer. Exhibited at the Tanner Gallery in November, with Otto van Rees, his first collages and his first tapestries. It was at this exhibition that he became acquainted with Sophie Taeuber. Artistic collaboration with Sophie Taeuber. Together they made horizontal and vertical collages, fabrics, tapestries.

1916–1919 Through the Hack bookshop he received a letter from Hugo Ball inviting him to join in the evenings of the "Cabaret Voltaire." With Ball, Emmy Hennings, Huelsenbeck, Janco, and Tzara, co-founder and leading participant in the "dada" movement of Zurich. Illustrated *Phantastische Gebete, Schalaben schalabai schalamezomai* by Huelsenbeck and *Vingt-cinq-et-un-poèmes* by Tzara (these three works in the Dada Collection). In the dadaist publications of Zurich, *Cabaret Voltaire, Dada 1–3, 391 (no. 8),* there appeared illustrations by Arp, and in *Dada 4–5* and *Der Zeltweg,* illustrations and poems.

1917 First abstract reliefs in wood.

1919–1920 In Cologne. Active participation with Baargeld and Max Ernst, in the dada movement of Cologne. Contributed in the dada publications of Cologne, *Die Schammade* and *Dada W/3*. Series of *Fatagaga* paintings with Max Ernst (Manufacture of paintings guaranteed to be gasometric.) Participated in the dada exhibition at the Brauhaus Winter, which was closed by the police. Trip to Berlin. Made the acquaintance of El Lissitzky, Kurt Schwitters, and the dada circle of Berlin. Exhibited at the "Erste Internationale Dada-Messe." Contributed to the *Dada-Almanach* of Richard Huelsenbeck. Published *die wolkenpumpe* (poems, at Paul Steegemann's, Hanover), *der vogel selbdritt* (poems and woodcuts, author's publication), and illustrated *Cinéma calendrier du coeur abstrait* by Tzara (Dada Collection. In stock at the Sans Pareil, Paris).

1921 With Eluard, Max Ernst, and Tzara at Tarrenz, in the Tyrol. Common publication: *Dada Au Grandair – Der Sängerkrieg Intirol.*

1922 Participated in the "International Dada Exhibition" at the Galerie Montaigne. Married Sophie Taeuber.

1923 In Hanover, at Kurt Schwitters'. Contributed to the reviews *Der Sturm* (Walden), *Mecano* (Van Doesburg), *Merz* (Schwitters). Published a series of lithographs, *7 Arpaden* (Merz publishing house).

1924 Published the collection of poems, *Der Pyramidenrock* (Eugen Rentsch Verlag, Erlenbach-Zurich). Contributed to the reviews *G* (Hans Richter), *De Stijl* (Van Doesburg).

1925 Editor, with El Lissitzky, of *Les Ismes de l'Art* (Eugen Rentsch, Erlenbach-Zurich). With Chirico, Max Ernst, Klee, Man Ray, Masson, Miro, Picasso, Pierre Roy, participated in the first exhibition of the surrealist group at the Galerie Pierre, Paris. Participated actively in the surrealist movement. Studio at 22 rue Tourlaque, near the studios of Max Ernst and Miro.

1926 Settled in Meudon. Made the acquaintance of Michel Seuphor.

1926–1928 Participated, with Theo van Doesburg and Sophie Taeuber, in the transformations of the "Aubette," in Strassburg.

1927 Contributed to the reviews *La Révolution Surréaliste* (Breton) and *Documents Internationaux de l'Esprit Nouveau* (Dermée and Seuphor). Exhibitions at the Galerie Surréaliste, Paris.

1929 Took part in the exhibition "Abstrakte und surrealistische Malerei und Plastik" at the Kunsthaus, Zurich.

1930 First torn papers. Publication of a collection of poems *Weisst du schwarzt du* (Pra Verlag, Zurich), and of *Konfiguration* (Poésie & Co., Paris). Member of the "Circle and Square" group founded by Seuphor. Participated in the exhibition organized by this group, Galerie 23, Paris.

1931–1932 First sculpture in the round. In 1932, member of the Abstraction-Création group, Paris. Contributed to the review *Transition* (Eugène Jolas). Exhibited at the Kunsthalle of Basel.

1936 Took part in the great exhibitions "Cubism and Abstract Art" and "Fantastic Art, Dada, Surrealism" at the Museum of Modern Art in New York. Member of the Swiss "Allianz" group.

1937–1939 Published the collections of poems *Des taches dans le vide* (Editions Sagesse, Paris, 1937), *Sciure de gamme* (Collection "Un Divertissement," Paris, 1938), and *Muscheln und Schirme* (published by the author, Meudon, 1939). Wrote a short novel, *L'homme qui a perdu son squelette* (Plastique No. 4–5) in collaboration with D. Carrington, Marcel Duchamp, Paul Eluard, Max Ernst, G. Hugnet, and G. Prassinos.

1940–1941 Southward exodus. Stay in Grasse with Sophie Taeuber, Sonia Delaunay, and Alberto Magnelli. Published the collection *Poèmes sans prénoms* (author's publication, Grasse, 1941).

1942 In the fall took refuge in Switzerland with Sophie Taeuber.

1943 Death of Sophie Taeuber in Zurich, January 13.

1944 Publication of collections of poems *1924–1925–1926–1943* (Verlag Benteli, Bern-Bümpliz) and *Rire de coquille* (Vordemberge-Gildewart, Amsterdam).

1945 The Editions Fontaine, Paris, published the collections of stories *Le blanc aux pieds de nègre* and *Trois nouvelles exemplaires* (in collaboration with Vicente Huidobro). The Allianz-Verlag, Zurich, published *11 Configurations* (11 woodcuts and texts by Arp, Bill, and G. Buffet-Picabia).

1946 Return to Meudon. The Editions Vrille, Paris, published the first complete collection of his poems in French: *Le Siège de l'air*.

1949 First voyage to America. Wittenborn and Schultz, New York, published the first important monograph on Arp: *On My Way – Poetry and Essays 1912–1947,* with texts by Arp, G. Buffet-Picabia, C. Giedion-Welcker, R. Motherwell, and a very extensive bibliography compiled by Bernard Karpel. One-man exhibition at Curt Valentin's, Buchholz Gallery, New York. Published *Onze peintres vus par Arp* (Editions Girsberger, Zurich). Took part in the exhibition "Premiers maîtres de l'art abstrait," Galerie Maeght, Paris, and contributed to Seuphor's book: *L'Art abstrait, ses origines, ses premiers maîtres* (published by Maeght).

1950 Second voyage to America. Executed a monumental wood relief for Harvard University in Cambridge. Exhibitions at the La Hune bookshop, Paris. A text by Michel Seuphor *Arcadie d'Arp* (first version) appeared on this occasion, accompanied by a bibliography. Published *Wegweiser – Jalons* (author's publication, Meudon) and *Auch das ist nur eine Wolke* (poems and 4 hand-colored cut-outs, Vineta-Verlag, Basel).

1952 Curt Valentin, New York, published *Dreams and Projects* (poetic texts and 28 woodcuts). Illustrated *Die New Yorker Kantaten* (Berggruen & Cie., Paris) and published *Die Engelsschrift* (poem to Sophie Taeuber, published by the author). First travel to Greece.

1953 Order for a monumental sculpture, *Shepherd of Clouds* (bronze, 10′ 6″ tall) for the Caracas Students' Residence Center. Publication of collections of poems *Behaarte Herzen, Könige vor der Sintflut* (Meta-Verlag, Frankfurt a. M.) and *Wortträume und schwarze Sterne* (Limes-Verlag, Wiesbaden). To this last collection he joined extensive marginal notes on his poetic work. Exhibition in Liège (with Sophie Taeuber). Michel Seuphor published *Mission spirituelle de l'Art, à propos de l'oeuvre de Sophie Taeuber-Arp et de Jean Arp* (Berggruen & Cie., Paris).

1954 Winner of the international prize of sculpture at the Venice Biennial. Illustrated the poems *Die Antwort der Tiefe* by Richard Huelsenbeck (Limes-Verlag, Wiesbaden). Participated, with a considerable personal contribution, in the exhibition "Seven Pioneers of Modern Sculpture," at Yverdon, an exhibition subsequently housed by the Kunsthaus of Zurich.

1955 Touring exhibition by Arp and Sophie Taeuber in Germany (Hanover, Berlin, Freiburg i. B.). The Limes-Verlag, Wiesbaden, published the collection of poems *Auf einem Bein* and the Verlag der Arche, Zurich, *Unsern täglichen Traum. Erinnerungen, Dichtungen und Betrachtungen aus den Jahren 1914–1954*. Illustrated A. M. Frey's collection *Kleine Menagerie* (Limes-Verlag, Wiesbaden). Second trip to Greece. Exhibition of reliefs at Edouard Loeb's, Paris, and of collages at Berggruen's, Paris.

1956 Large Arp-Schwitters exhibition at the Kunsthalle of Berne. First execution of the *Arpiade,* Wladimir Vogel's cantata on eight of Arp's poems.

1957 Exhibitions at the galleries Naviglio, Milan, Cavallino, Venice, and Selecta, Rome. Work on a monumental bronze relief for the Unesco Building in Paris.

Lives in Meudon.

Hans Bolliger

Forest – 1916 – Painted wood – 12⁵/₈ × 8¹/₄″

Earth Forms, also called Enak's Tears – 1916/1917 – Painted wood – 16 1/2 × 11″

Plant Hammer – 1917 – Painted wood – 24³⁄₄ × 19⁵⁄₈″

Mask – 1918 – Wood – 11 × 12³/₄"

Bird Mask – 1918 – Wood

Egg Board – 1922 – Painted wood – 29 ¹/₂ × 39″

Madame Torso with Wavy Hat – 1916 – Wood – 15⁷/₈ × 10³/₈″

Torso – 1925 – Wood – 9 1/2 × 6 3/4″

Shirt Front and Fork – 1924 – Painted wood – ca. 23⁵/₈ × 23⁵/₈″

Mountain Table Anchors Navel – 1926 – Painted cardboard – 29⁵/₈ × 23¹/₂″

Eye and Navel Dress – 1925 – Painted cardboard

Configuration, also called Navel Shirt and Head – 1926 – Painted plywood – 56 ¹/₄ × 44 ¹/₂″

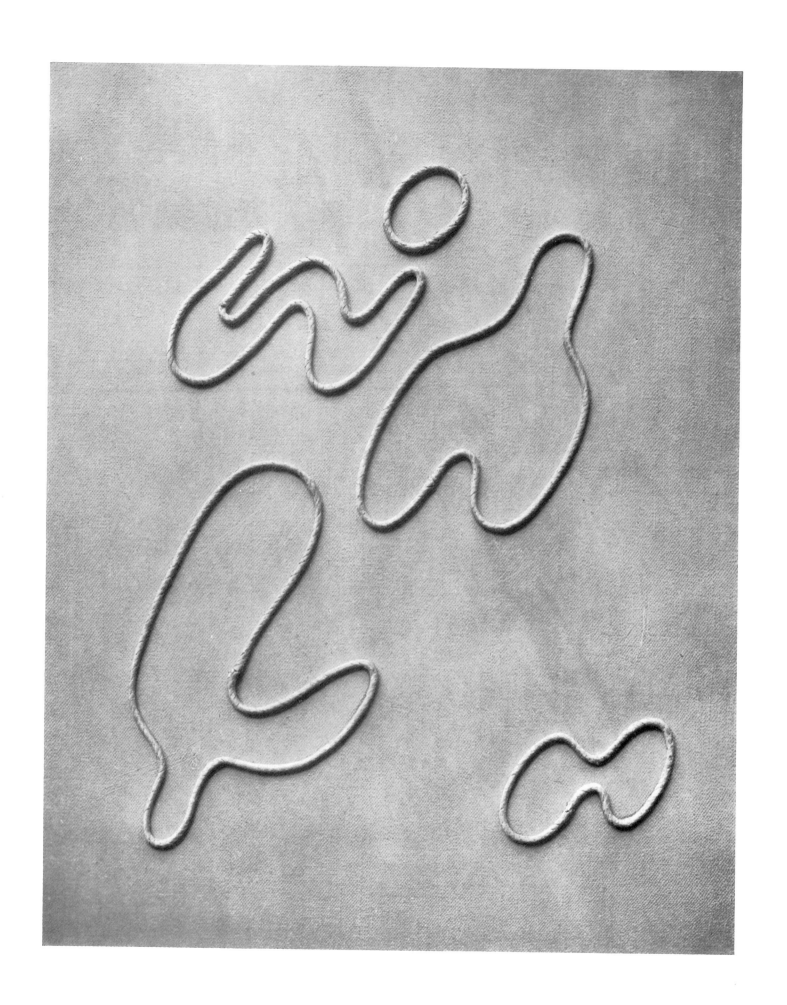

Objects Arranged as Writing – 1928 – String relief – 22 × 18⁷/₈"

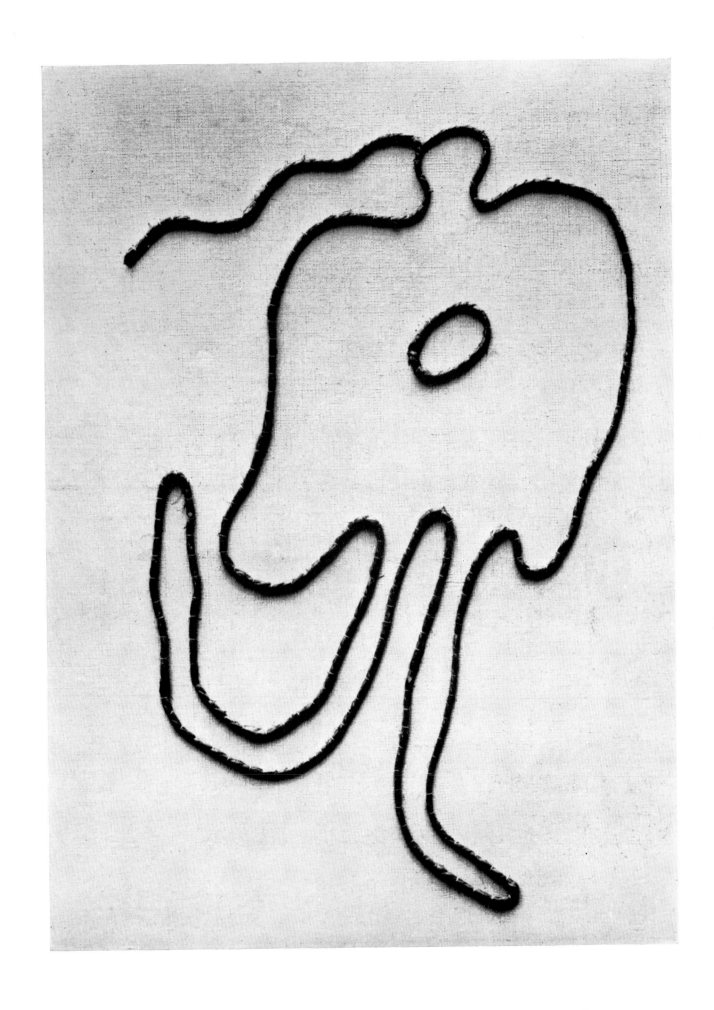

Dancer – 1928 – String relief – 19⁵/₈ × 15³/₄″

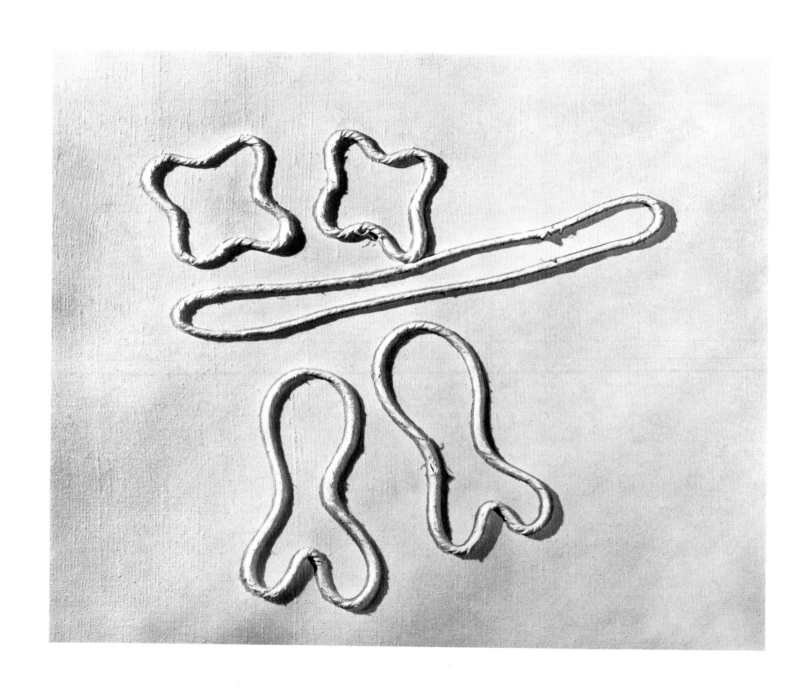

Enigmatic Account – 1928 – String relief

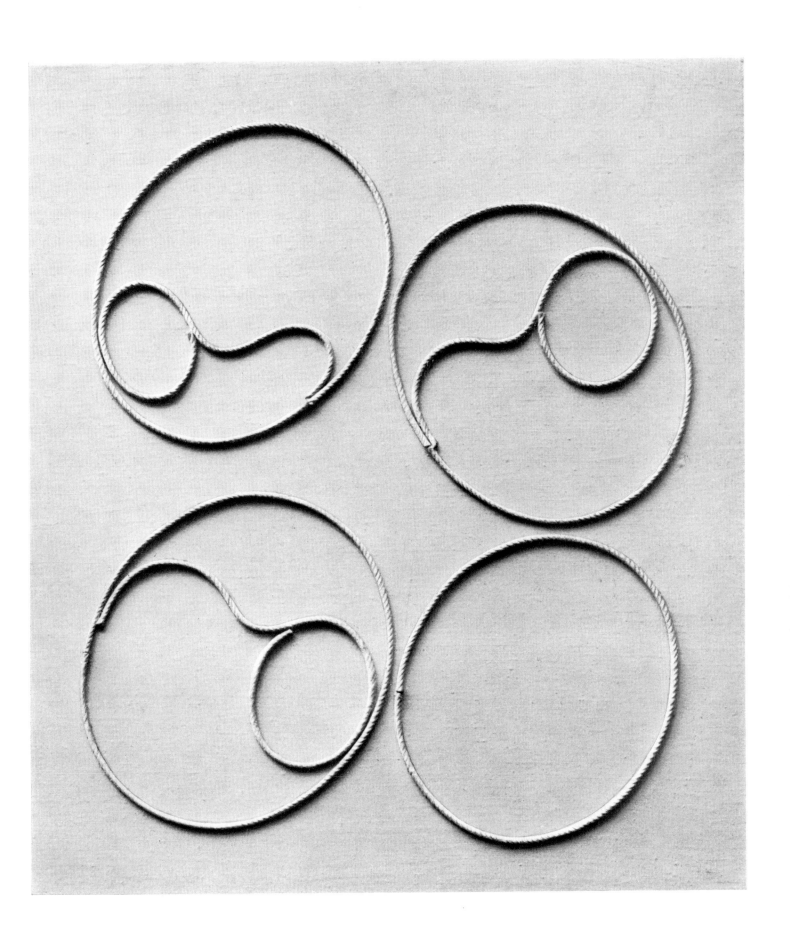

Composition with Circles – 1930 – String relief – 21 $^1/_4$ × 19 $^1/_4$ ″

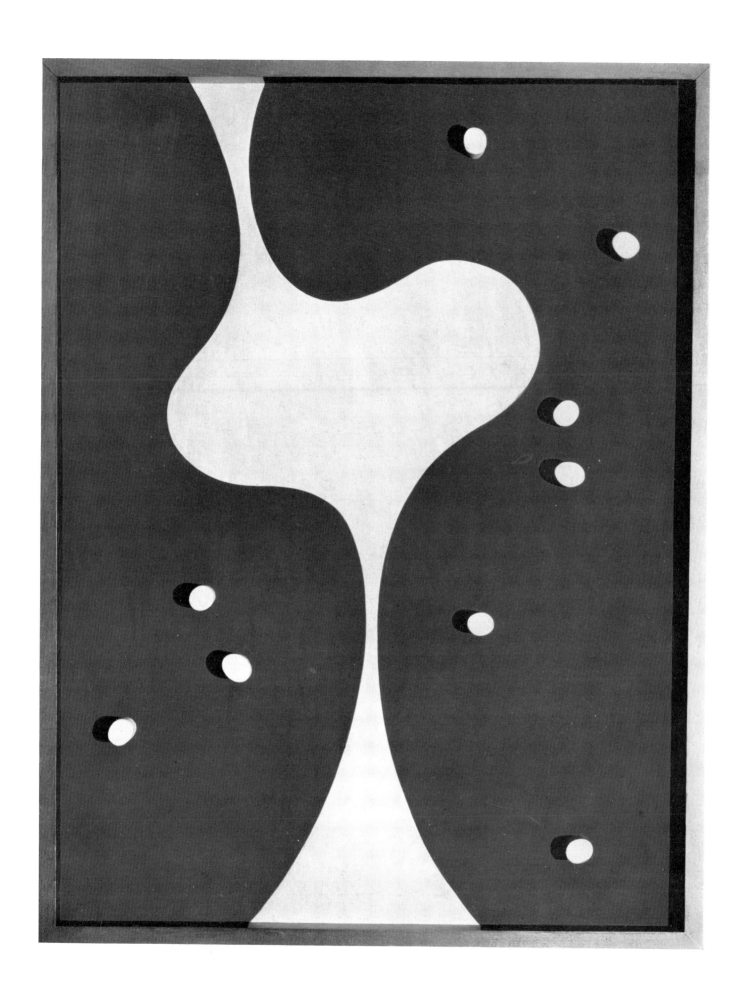

Amphora – 1931 – Painted wood – 55¹/₈ × 43¹/₄″

Infinite Amphora – 1929 – Painted wood – 57 ¹/₈ × 44 ⁷/₈″

Forks and Navel – 1927 – Painted wood – 39³/₈ × 51¹/₈″

Mythical Composition – 1929/1952 – Painted wood – 55 1/8 × 43 1/4"

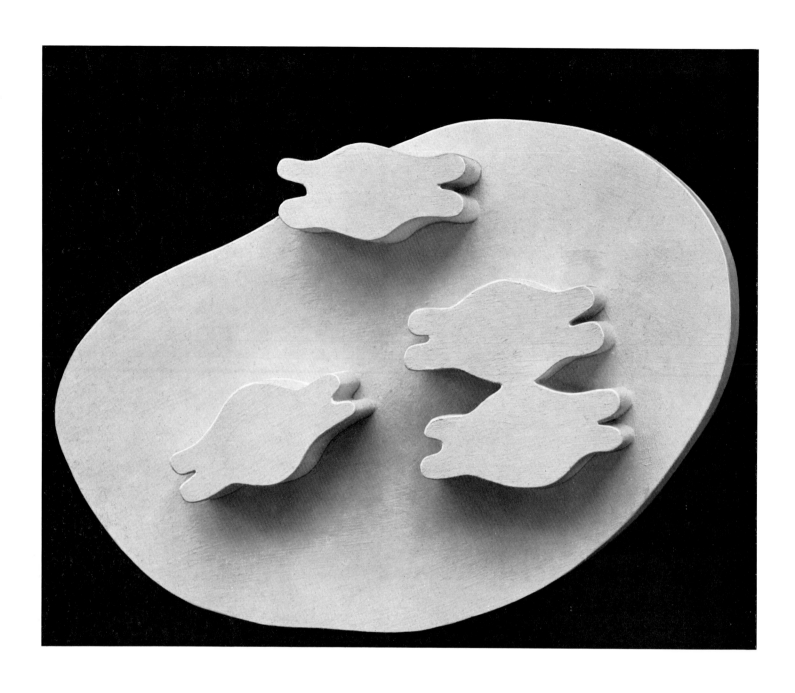

Flight of Birds – 1930 – Painted wood

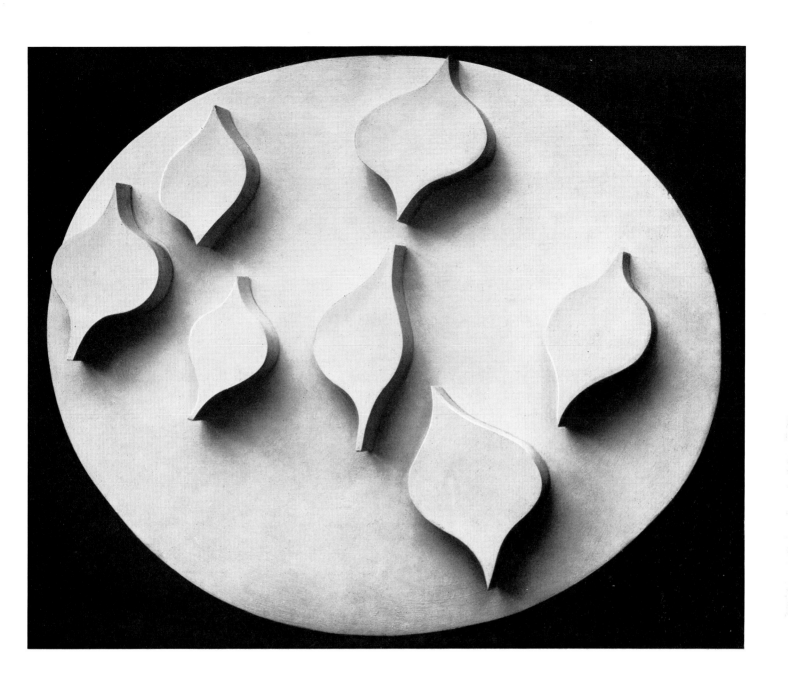

Constellation of Leaves on Oval Form – 1930 – Painted wood – 19 × 23³/₄″

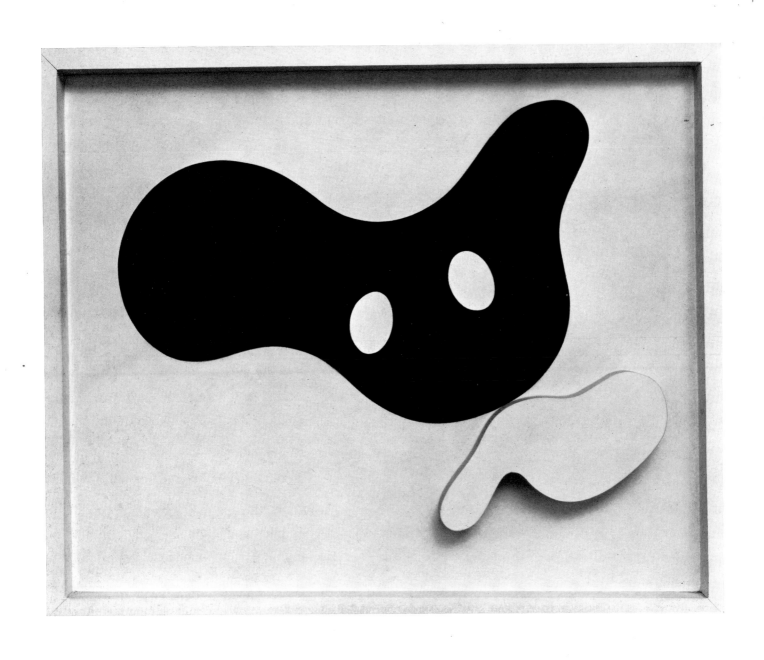

Masked Play – 1932 – Painted wood – 27$^{1}/_{8}$ × 33$^{1}/_{2}$"

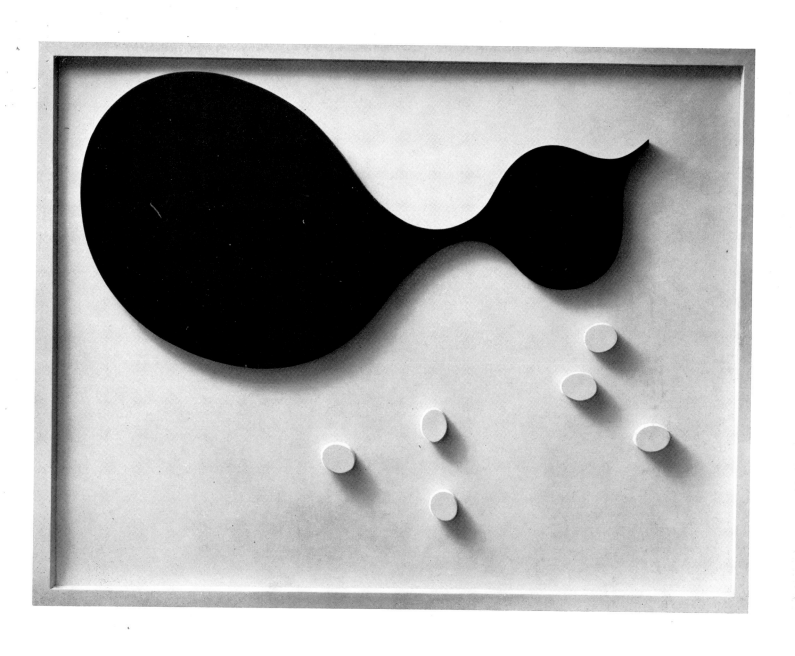

Arrow Cloud – 1932 – Painted wood – 43 $^1/_4$ × 55 $^1/_8$"

According to the Laws of Chance – 1931 – Wood – 10¹/₄ × 11″

Configuration with Two Dangerous Points – 1932 – Painted wood – 25⅝ × 33⅛″

Arranged According to the Laws of Chance – 1929 – Painted wood – 55 ¹/₈ × 42 ¹/₈″

According to the Laws of Chance, also called Periods and Commas – 1944 – Painted wood – 43 ¹/₄ × 55 ¹/₈″

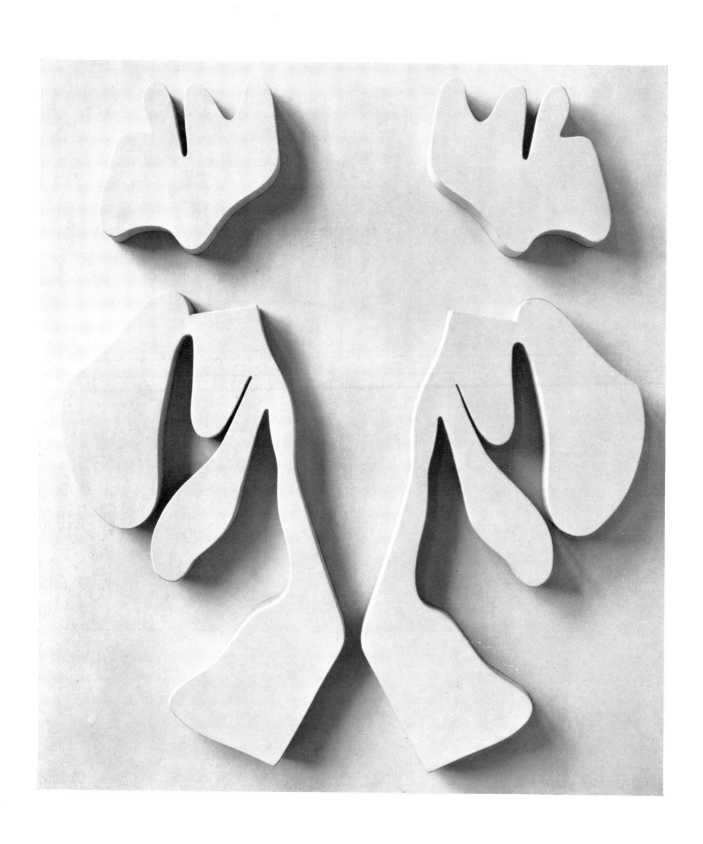

Vegetal Symmetry – 1946 – Natural wood – 21⁵/₈ × 19¹/₄″

Summer Metope

1946 – Oak wood –55⁷/₈ × 25⁵/₈″

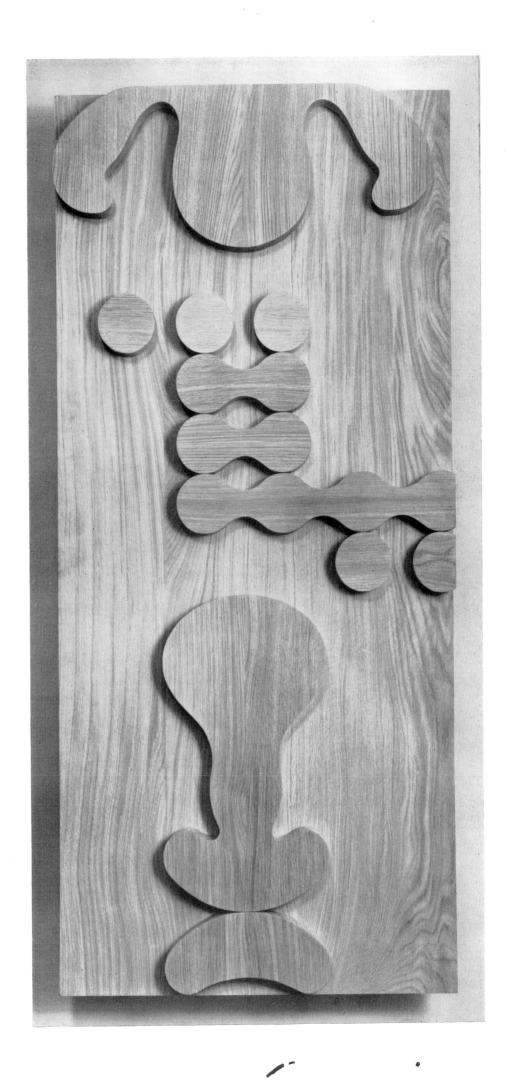

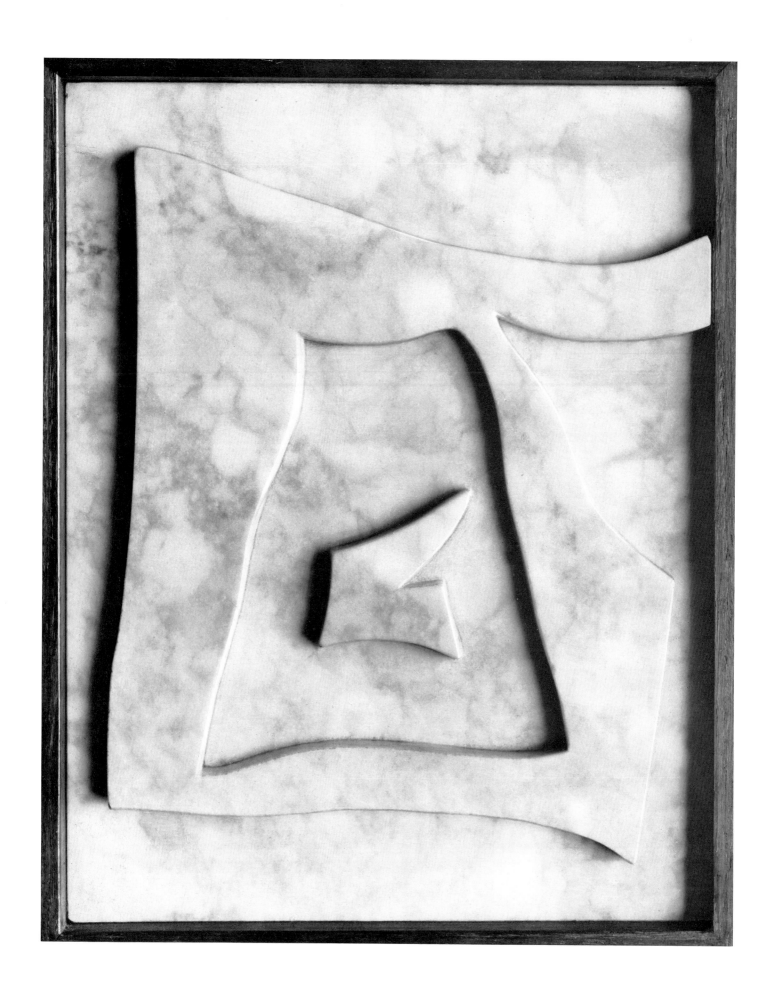

Mediterranean Initial – 1941 – Marble – 10³/₄ × 8¹/₄″

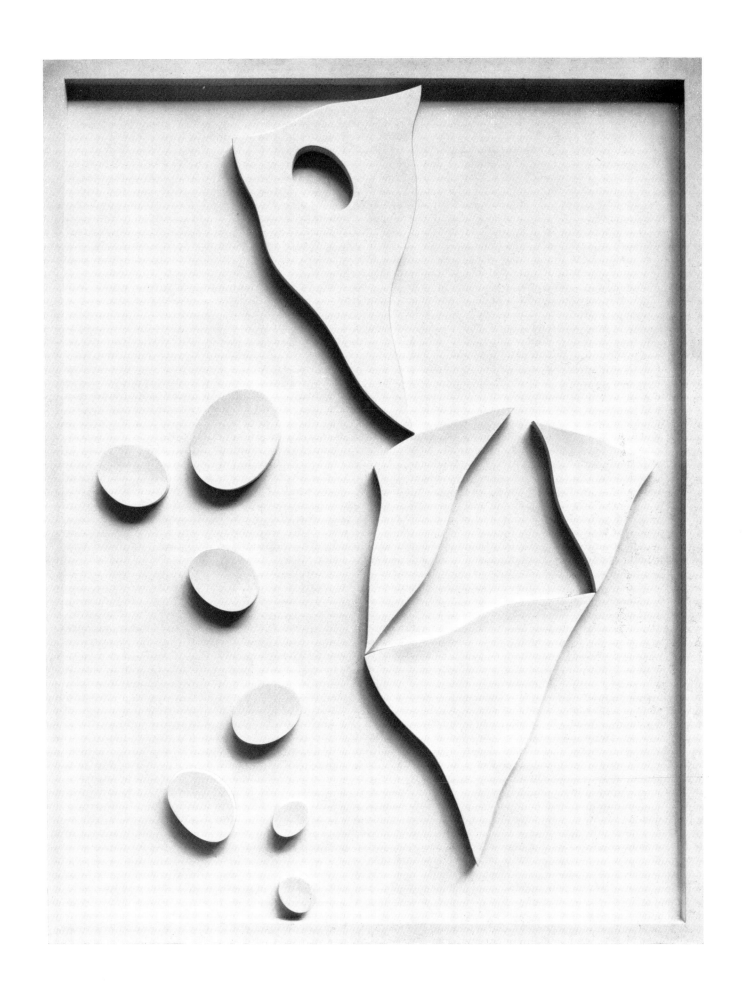

Structure of White Blossoms for my Dead Wife – 1943 – Wood – 55 1/8 × 43 3/4"

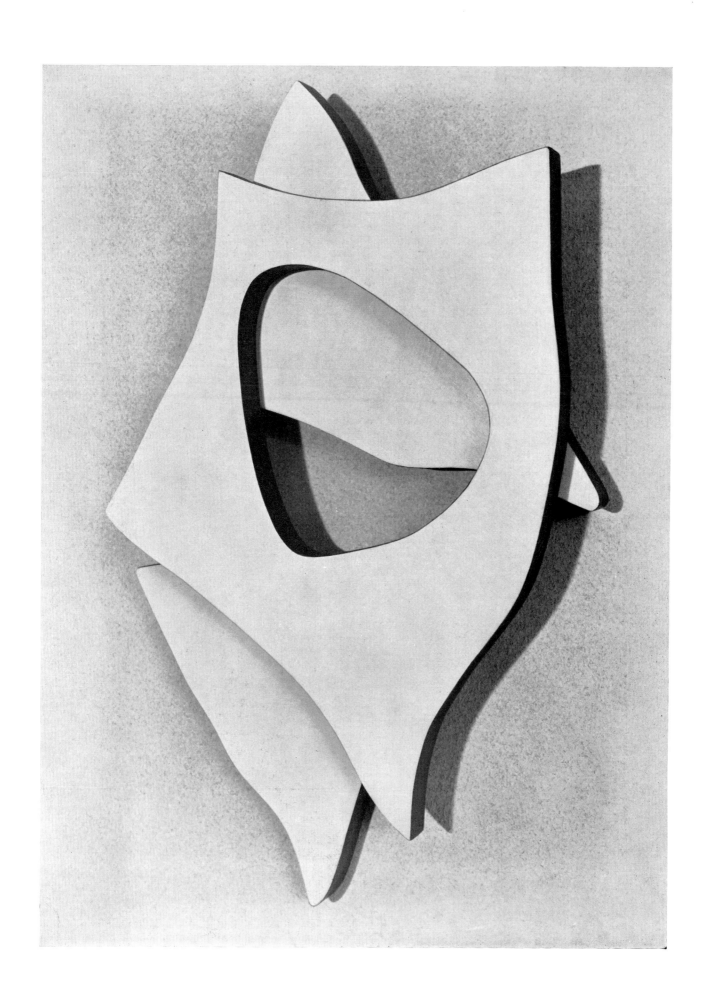

Vegetal Pendulum, also called Leafy Glance – 1944 – Painted wood – 23⁵/₈ × 15³/₄″

Vegetal Coat-of-Arms – 1944 – Painted wood – 18⁷/₈ × 15³/₄″

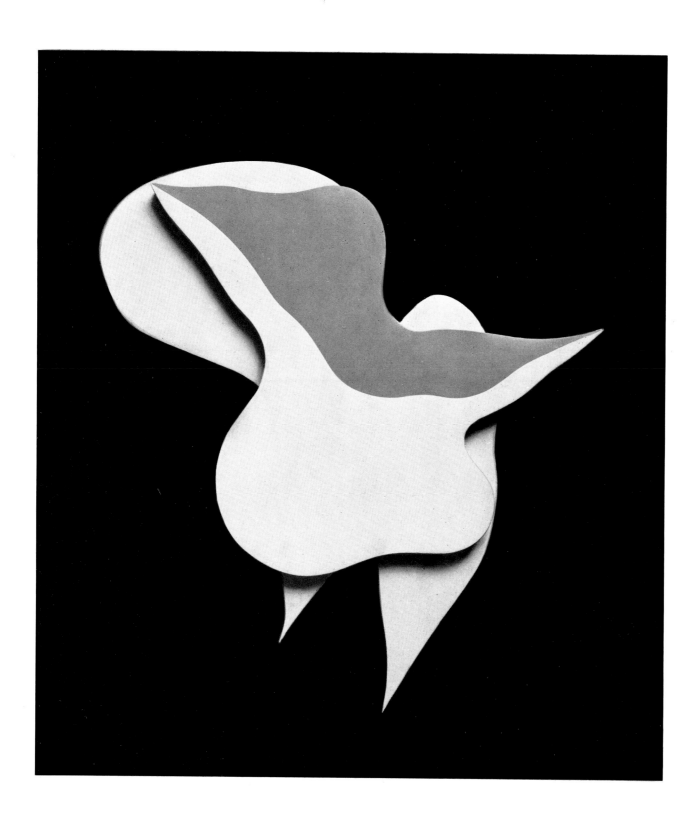

Birdlike Cloud – 1943 – Painted wood – 19 × 17"

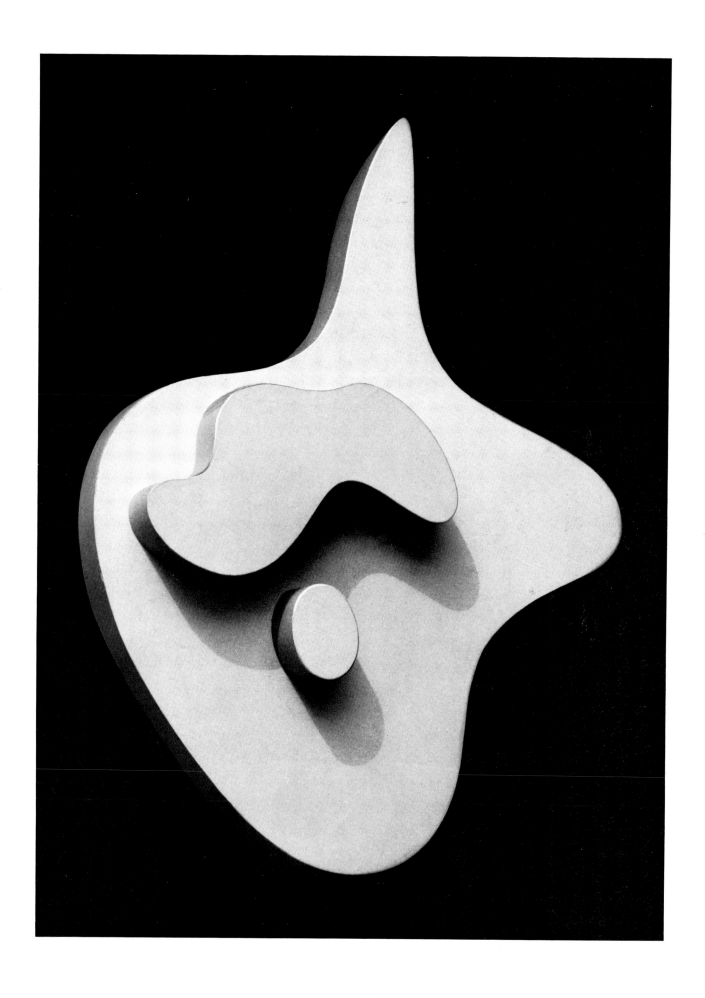

Calendar Clock – 1944 – Painted wood – 18⁷/₈ × 16¹/₈″

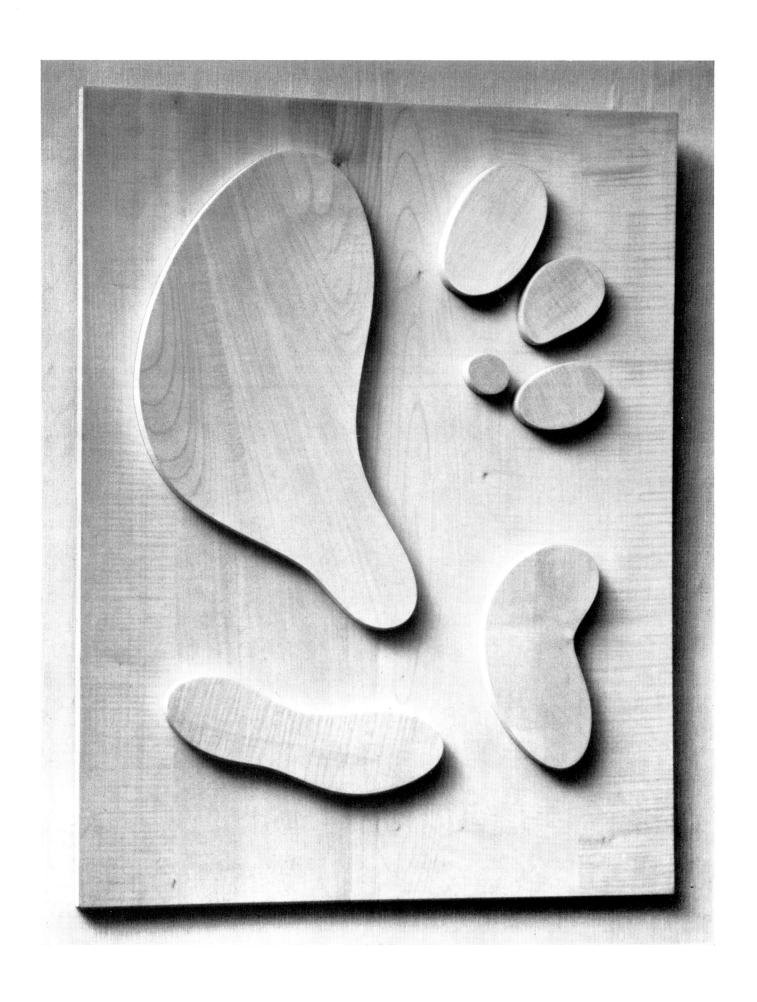

Constellation of Neutral Forms – 1953 – Polished natural wood – 29 ¹/₂ × 23 ⁵/₈"

Genesis – 1945 – Painted wood – 33¹/₈ × 29¹/₈″

Interregnum – 1949 – Cardboard relief – 11 × 7⁷/₈″

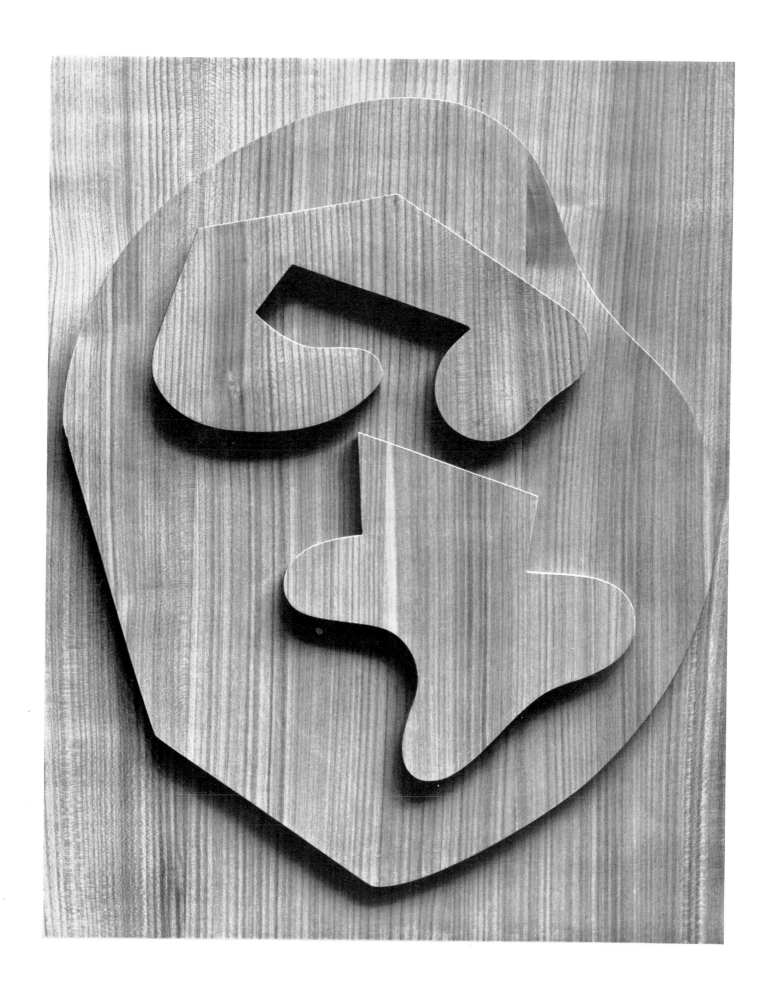

Before the Birth of Music – 1951 – Cherry wood – 21 ¹/₄ × 17 ³/₈″

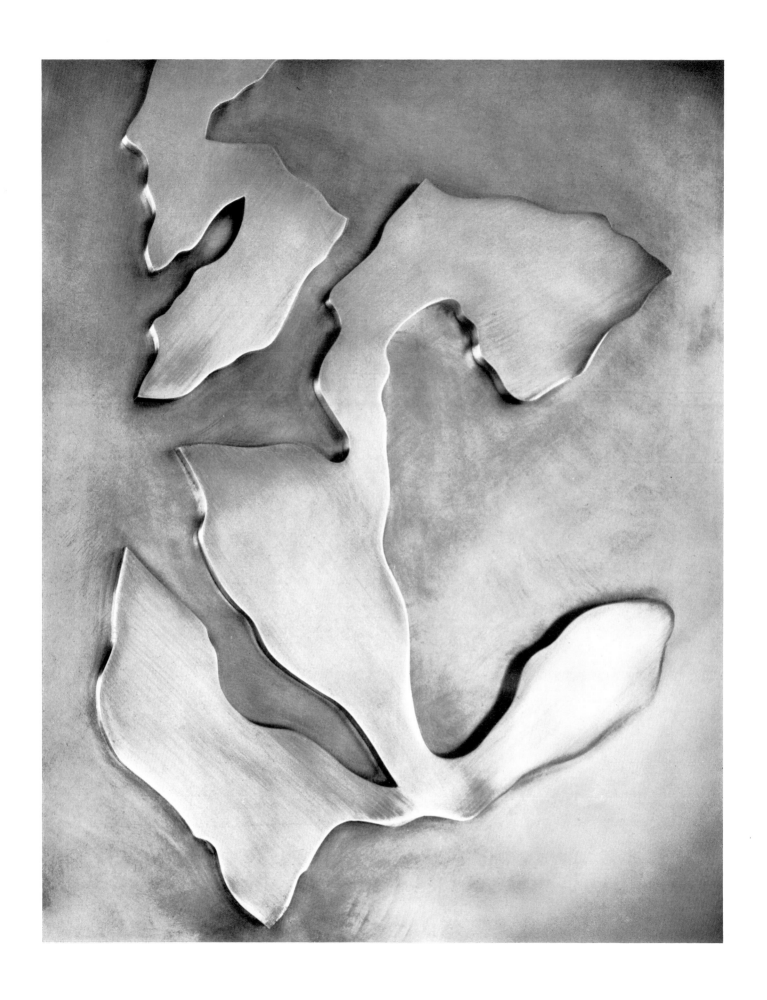

Configuration: Memory of Athens – 1955 – Bronze – 29$^1/_8$ × 23$^1/_4$″

43

Configuration – *1955* – *Bronze* – *19⁵/₈ × 15³/₄″*

Shell Profiles – 1930 – Painted wood – 26³/₈ × 29⁷/₈ × 20¹/₂″

Hand Fruit – 1930 – Painted wood – 21⁵/₈ × 34⁵/₈ × 7⁷/₈″

Figures, One Large and Two Small – 1931 – Painted wood – 24³/₄ × 17³/₄ × 17³/₄″

Bell and Navels – 1931 – White-painted wood – 10 ¹/₄ × 19 ¹/₄″

To Be Exposed in the Woods (sculpture in three forms) – 1932 – Bronze –
large 1¹/₂ × 8³/₄ × 5¹/₂"; medium 2³/₄ × 4³/₄ × 3⁷/₈"; small 2 × 3⁵/₈ × 2³/₈"

49

Head with Annoying Objects – 1930 – Plaster – Face 14¹/₈ × 10¹/₄ × 7¹/₂″;
Mustache 5³/₈ × 4 × 3¹/₈″; Mandolin 5¹/₈ × 2³/₈ × 2″; Fly 6¹/₄ × 2⁷/₈ × 4³/₄″

Giant Seed – 1936 – Limestone – 59 × 43¹/₄ × 39³/₈″

Pagoda Fruit – 1949 – Bronze – 55 ¹/₈ × 27 ⁵/₈ × 25 ⁵/₈″

Human Concretion – 1935 – Limestone – 28 ³/₄ × 19 ¹/₄ × 17 ³/₄″ →

Gnome, also called Kaspar – 1930 – Plaster – 19⁵/₈ × 11 × 7¹/₂″

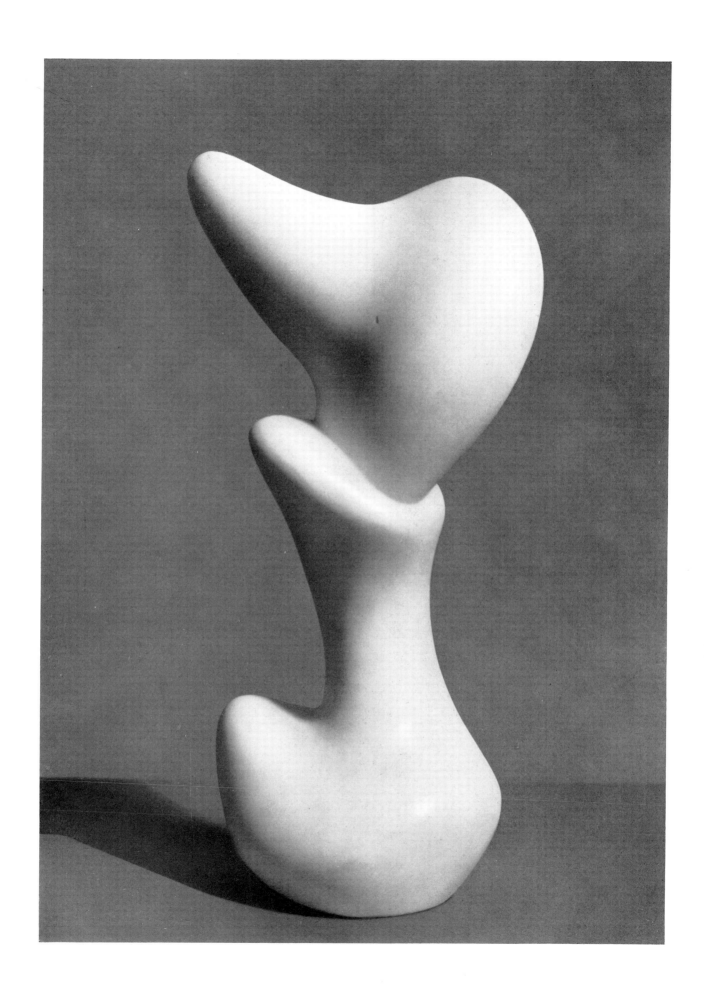

Bust of Gnome – 1949 – Marble – 12³/₈ × 5⁵/₈ × 3⁷/₈"

Little Sphinx – 1942 – Bronze – $7^1/_2 \times 16^1/_8 \times 4^3/_8{}''$

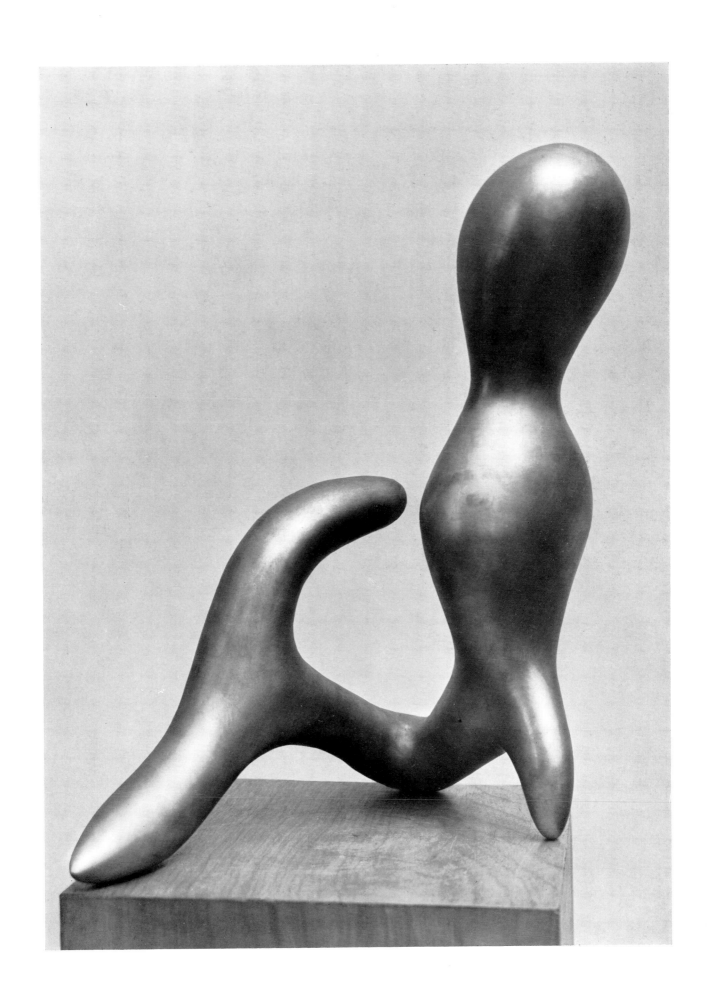

Siren – 1942 – Bronze – 17³/₄ × 13³/₈ × 9¹/₈″

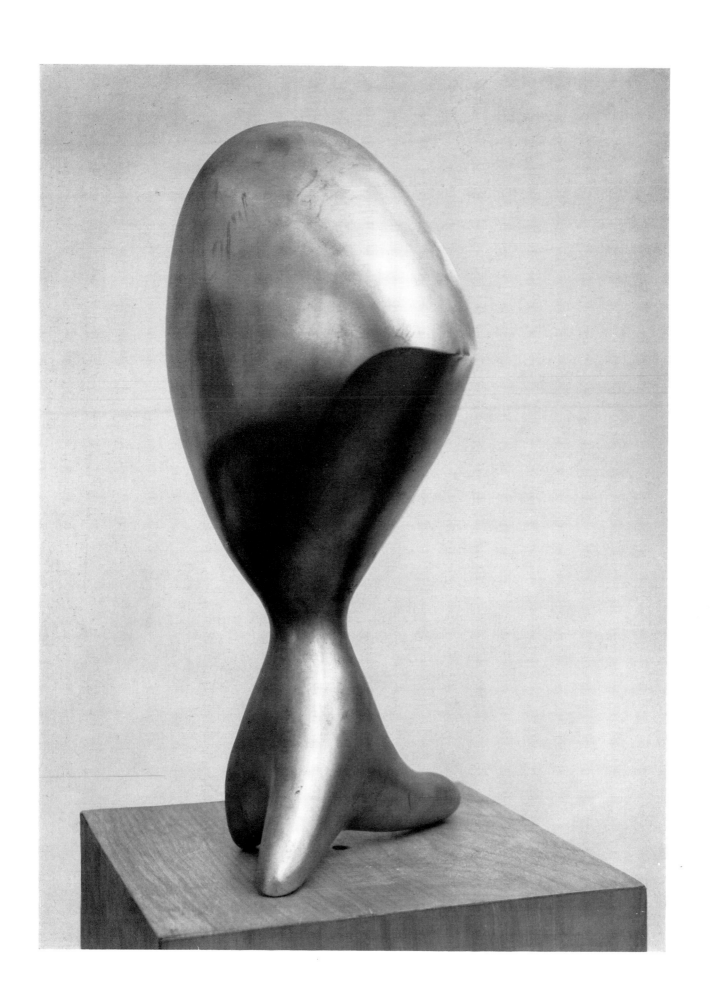

Head with Claws – 1949 – Bronze – 18¹⁄₂ × 9 × 7¹⁄₂″

Cup with Small Chimera – 1947 – Bronze – 31 ¹/₂ × 17 ³/₈ × 12 ⁵/₈ ″

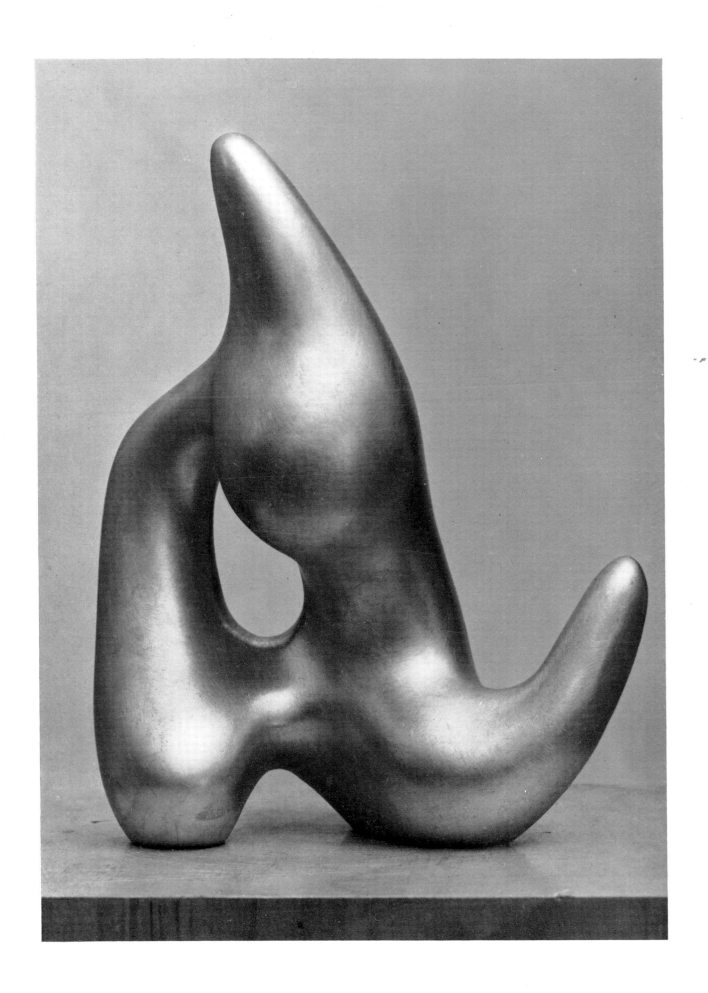

From Gnomeland – 1949 – Bronze – 9⁷/₈ × 8 × 3⁷/₈"

Shepherd of Clouds – 1953 – Plaster – 10′ 6″ × 48³/₈″ × 7′ 2⁵/₈″ – Yverdon Castle, Switzerland

Stone Formed by Human Hand – 1937/1938 – Jura limestone – 16¹/₄ × 19⁵/₈ × 9⁷/₈"

Growth

1938 – Bronze – 31 $^1/_2$ × 9 $^7/_8$ × 12 $^5/_8$″

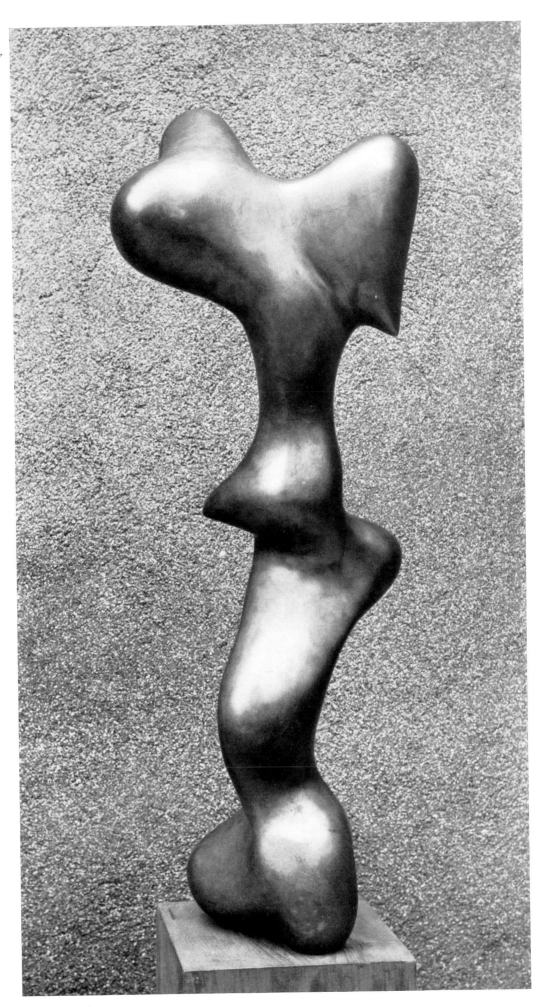

63

Metamorphosis (Shell – Swan – Swing) – 1935 – Bronze – 27¹/₈ × 18¹/₈ × 16"

Page 65, above: Pagan Stone – 1942 – Black granite – 5⁷/₈ × 10¹/₂ × 4³/₄"

below: Snake Bread – 1942 – Black granite – 6¹/₄ × 10¹/₄ × 6¹/₄"

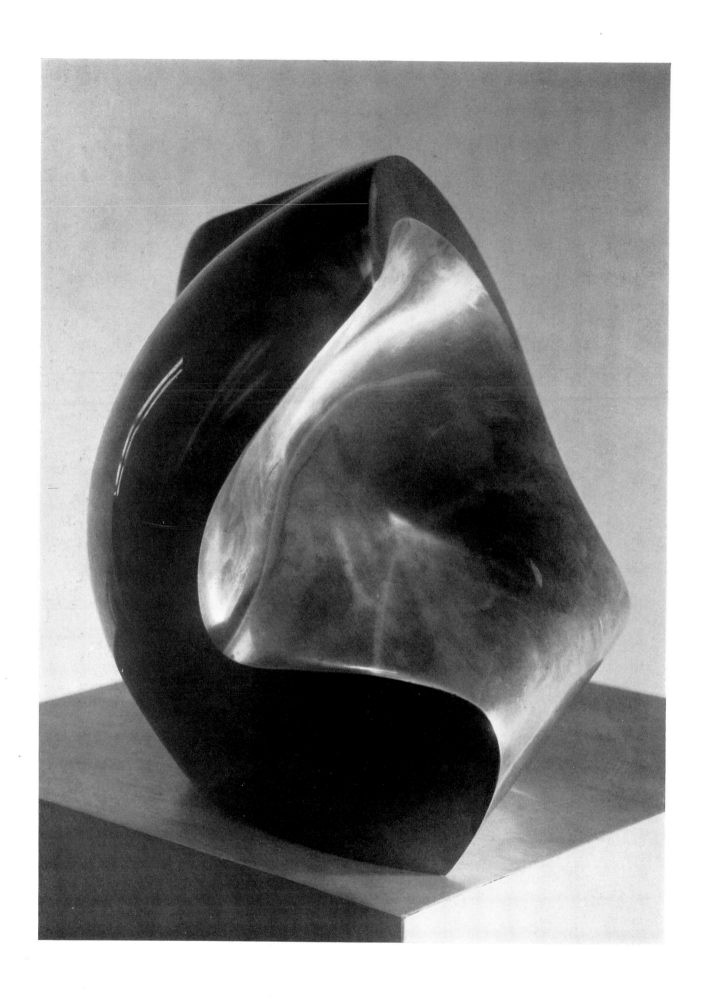

Shell – 1938 – Bronze – 9 × 11 × 8¹/₄″

Cyprian Sculpture – 1951 – White marble – 15³/₄ × 22⁵/₈ × 12³/₄″

Leaf – 1941 – White marble – 16 ⁷/₈ × 9 ⁵/₈ × 9 ⁵/₈"

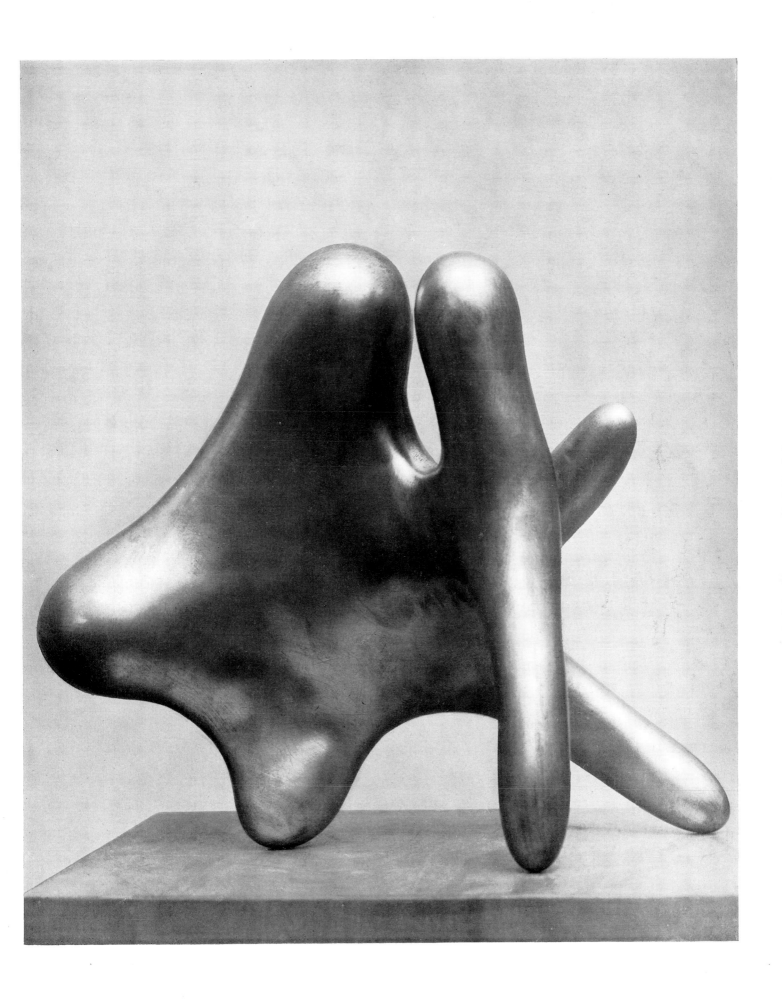

Mediterranean Group – 1941/1942 – Bronze – 8¹/₄ × 11⁷/₈ × 6⁷/₈"

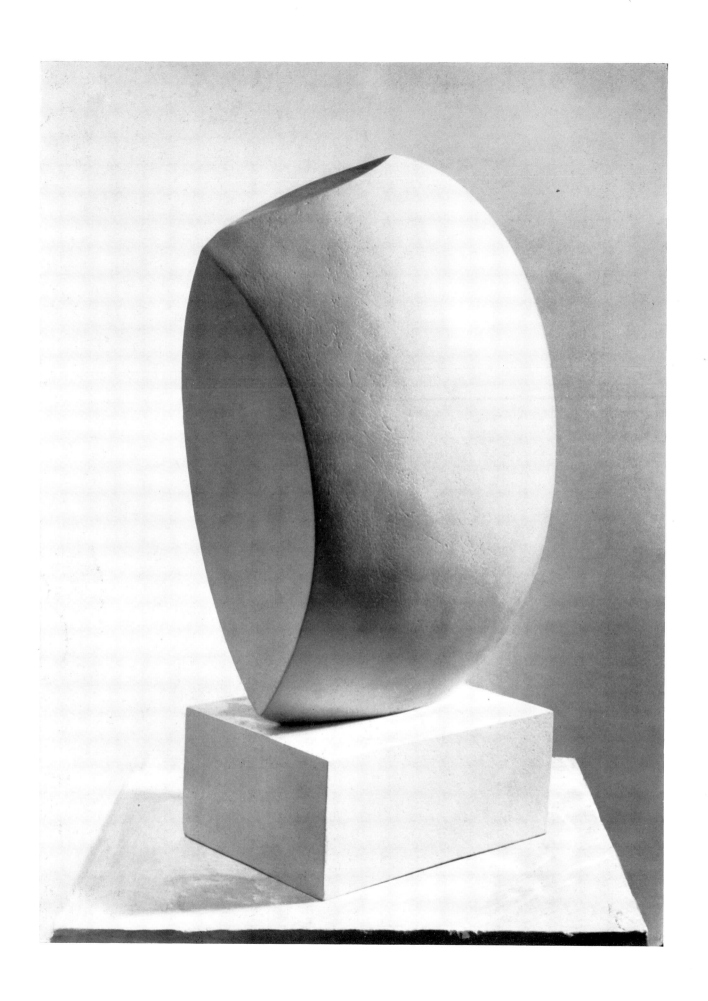

Mediterranean Sculpture I, also called Orphic Dream – 1941 – Terracotta – 15 × 10⁵/₈ × 6³/₈"

Mediterranean Sculpture I, also called Orphic Dream

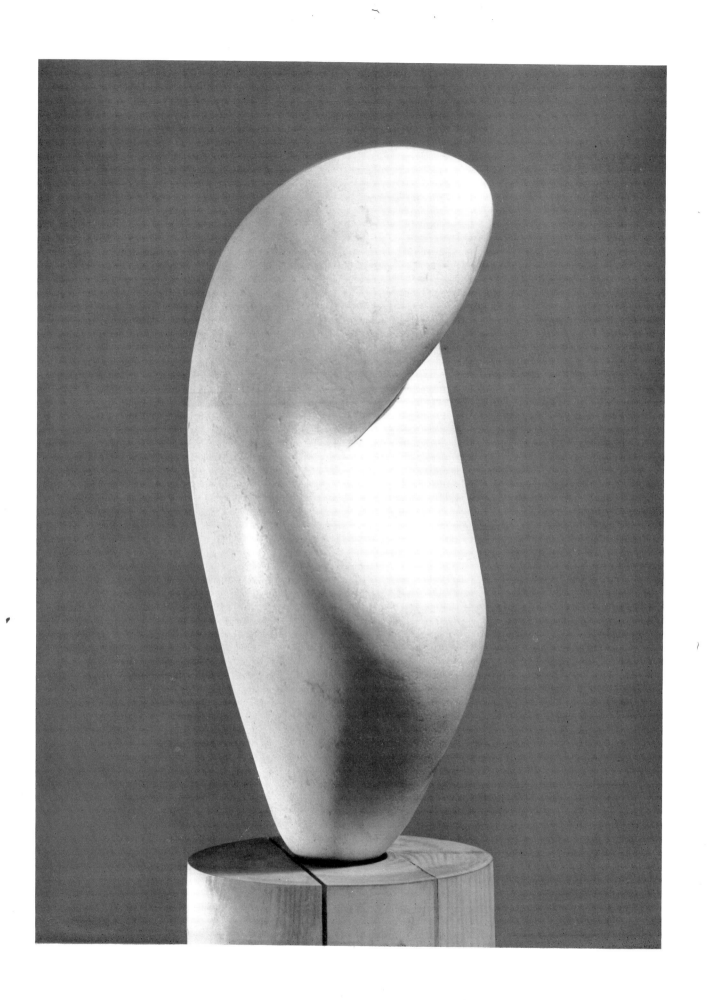

Owl's Dream – 1951 – Marble – 15³/₄ × 9 × 7⁷/₈"

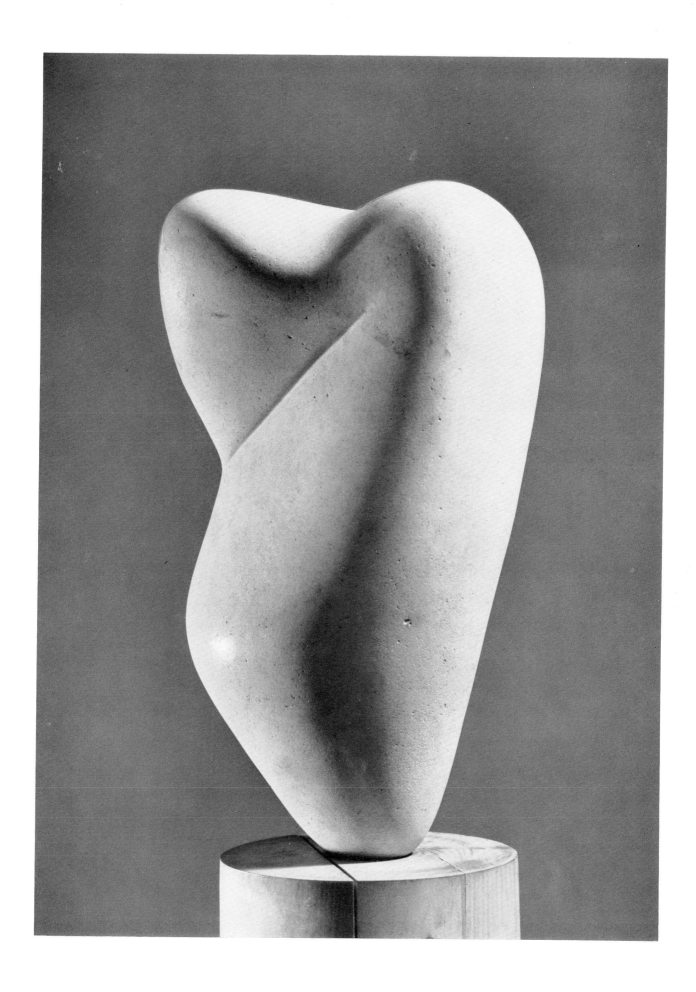

Owl's Dream

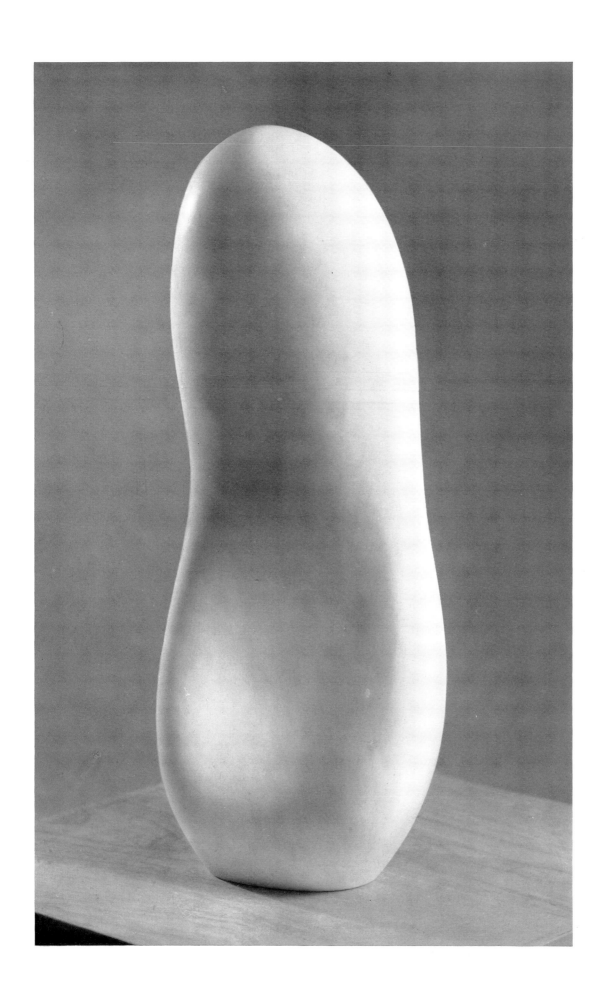

Silent – 1942 – White marble – 13³/₈ × 5¹/₂ × 4³/₈"

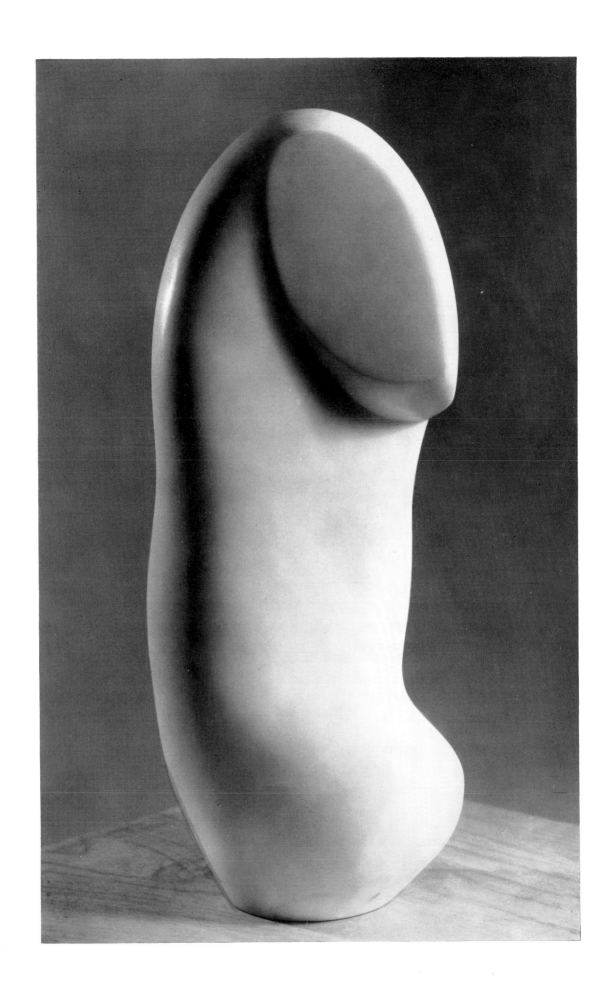

Concrete Form from Two Realms – 1942 – White marble – 14¹/₈ × 5¹/₂ × 5¹/₂″

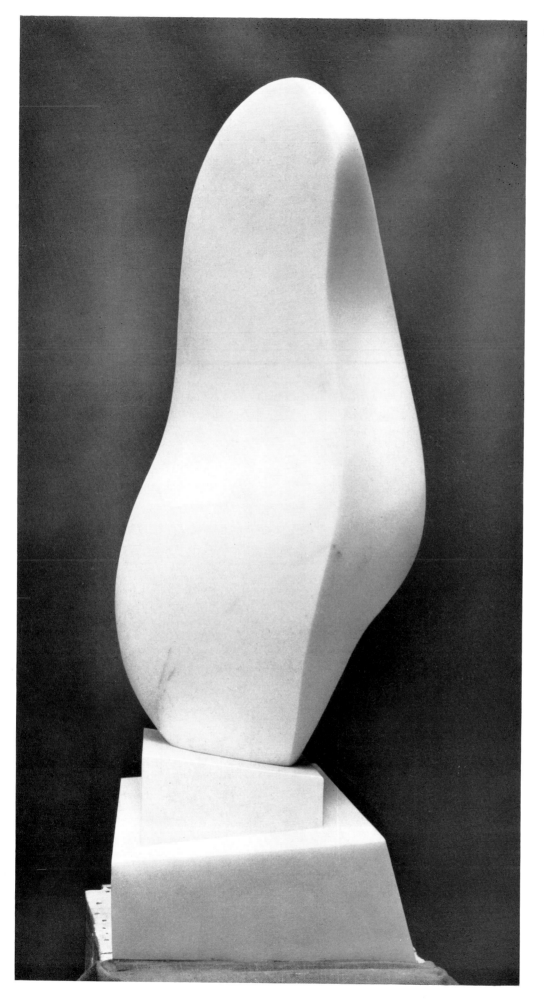

Leaf on Crystal – 1954
White marble – $17^7/_8 \times 9^1/_2 \times 8^5/_8''$

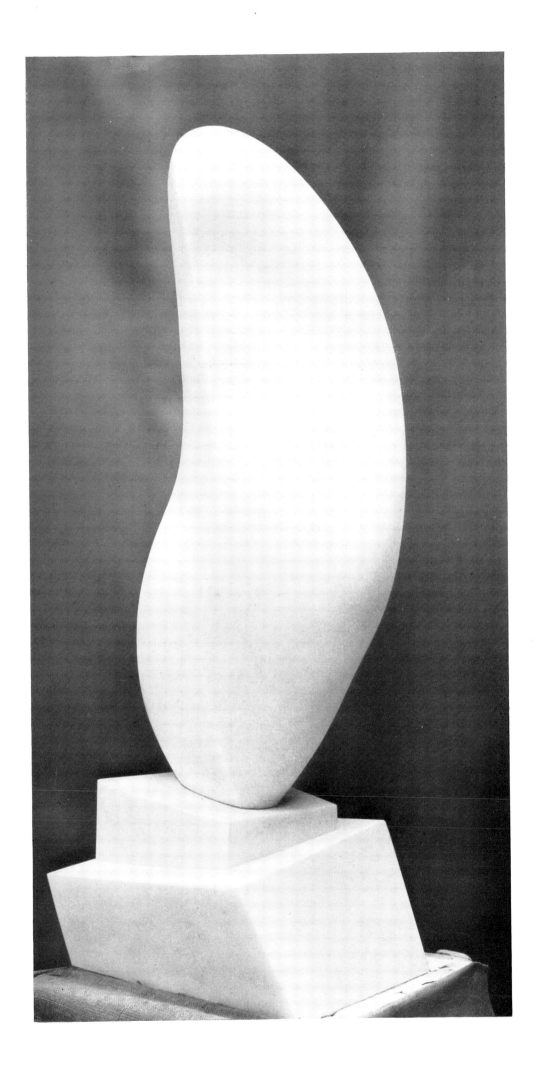

← Geometric-Ageometric – 1942 – Bronze – 11³/₈ × 11¹/₈ × 6³/₈″

Oru – 1953 – White marble – 8⁵/₈ × 11³/₄ × 15³/₄″ →

Shell Crystal – 1938 – Bronze – 10⁵/₈ × 14⁵/₈ × 15″

Shell Crystal

Tree of Bowls – 1947 – Bronze – 39 ³/₈ × 19 ⁵/₈"

Tree of Bowls

Snake Movement I – 1950 – White marble – 8¹/₄ × 13³/₈ × 11³/₈″

Snake Movement II – 1955 – Concrete stone – 17³/₈ × 29¹/₈ × 22⁷/₈″

Torso – 1931 – Marble
24 × 16 × 7¹/₄″; base 14¹/₈ × 10¹/₂ × 7¹/₈″

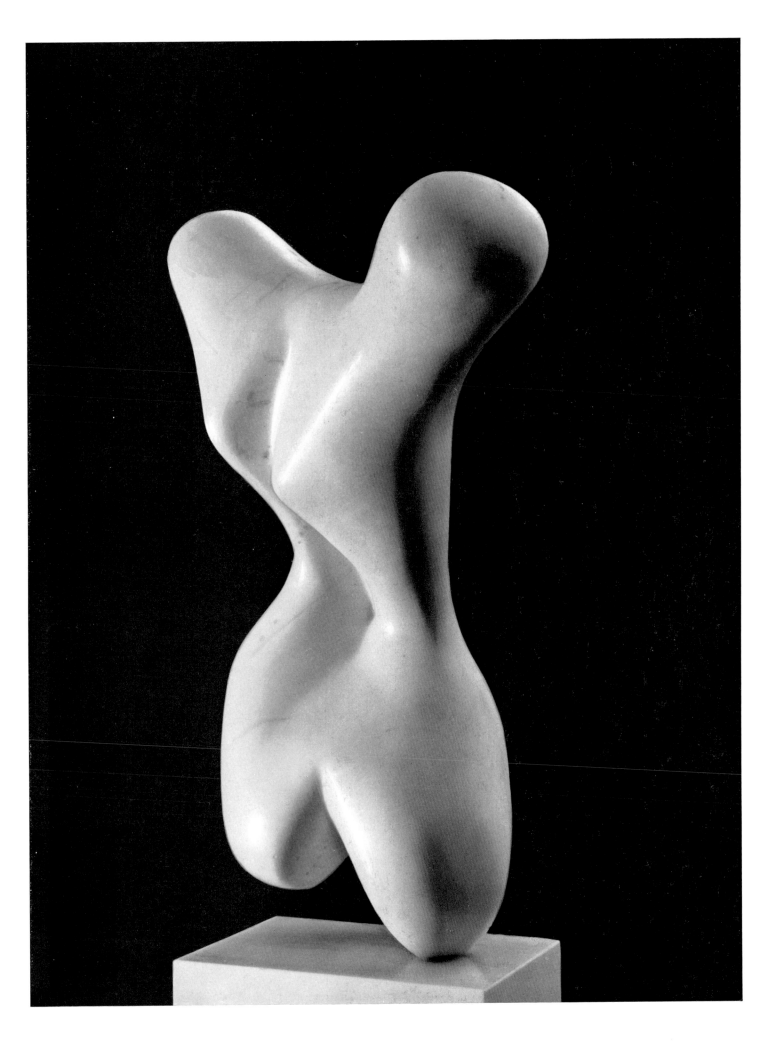

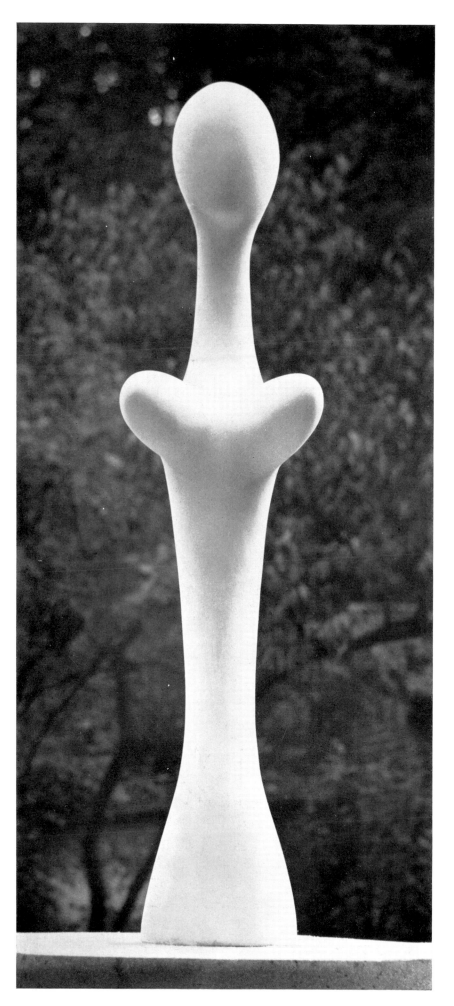

Small Mythical Figure
1950 – Plaster – 28 × 6³/₈ × 6⁷/₈″

Idol – 1950 – Plaster – 42⁷/₈ × 15 × 8¹/₄″

Human Lunar Spectral – 1950 – White marble on base – 36⁵/₈ × 25⁵/₈ × 19⁵/₈″

Human Lunar Spectral – *1950* – *Pink limestone* – *$32^5/_8 \times 25^5/_8 \times 19^5/_8$″*

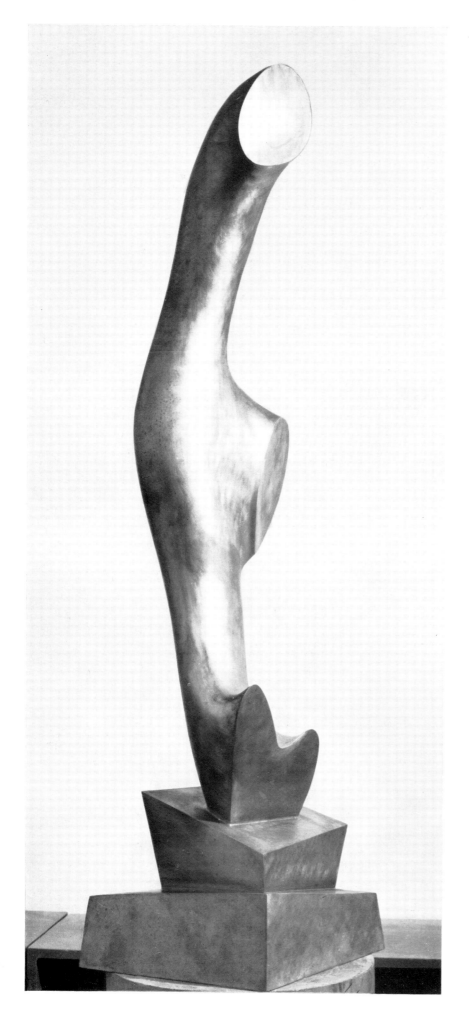

Daphne

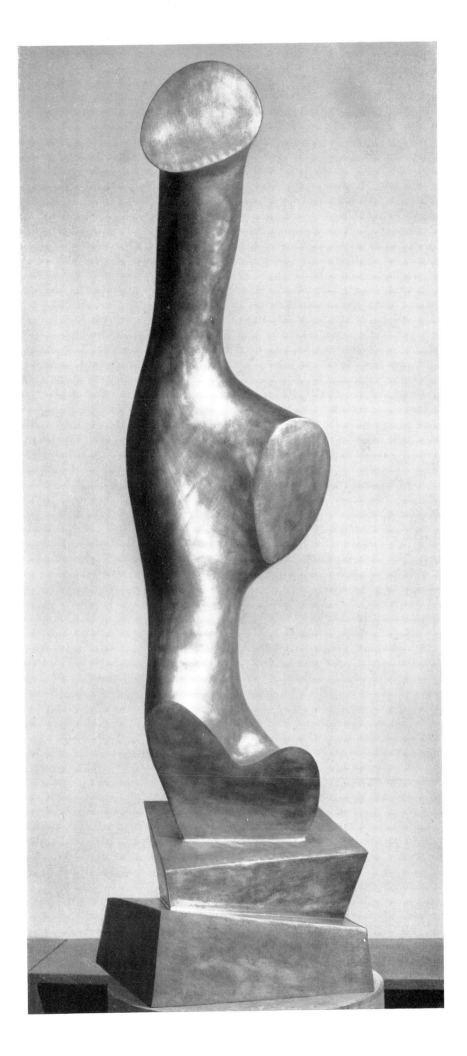

Star – 1939 – Bronze on stone base – 4⁵/₈ × 6³/₈ × 1³/₄″; base 5¹/₈″ × 4³/₈″

Garland of Buds – 1936 – Pink limestone – 18⁷/₈ × 15 × 11³/₈″

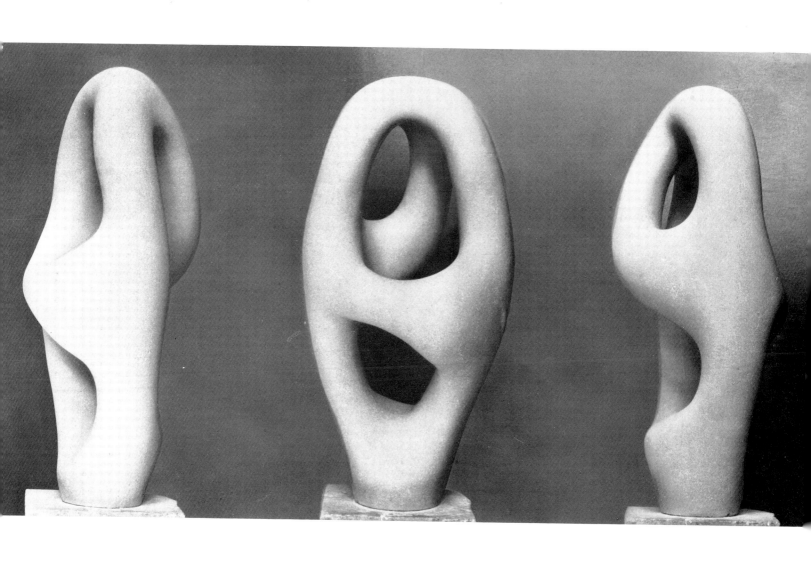

Ptolemy – 1953 – Limestone (Euville) – 40 ¹/₂ × 20 ⁷/₈ × 16 ⁷/₈″

Ptolemy – Bronze

Rising Navel and Two Heads – 1927/1928 – Mural painting – Aubette, Strassburg (destroyed)

Head with Mustache – 1927/28
Mural painting – Aubette, Strassburg (destroyed)

Navel-Sun – 1927/28 – Mural painting – Aubette, Strassburg (destroyed)

Constellation – 1950 – Wood relief – Harvard Graduate Center

Configuration – 1956 – Metal on cement – Ciudad Universitaria, Caracas, Venezuela

List of Reproductions

* The H-numbers in parentheses refer to Marguerite Hagenbach's Catalogue of Sculptures (see p. 108).

Illustrations in Text

Catalogue of Sculptures

Since Jean Arp has never kept records of his artistic production or his sales, I have not had time to prepare a complete catalogue of his works. I have therefore confined myself to listing the sculptures done after 1930, and I have not included his extraordinarily numerous and varied reliefs, paintings, embroideries, collages, string reliefs, and other works. In the bibliography the reader will find many graphic works mentioned, and a noteworthy selection of his reliefs, string reliefs, and collages is reproduced in this book. I hope that my preliminary effort will induce a student of art history to undertake a complete catalogue, which, even though it requires a great deal of research, and hence of time, would in my opinion be an interesting and rewarding task,

for only such a catalogue will clearly demonstrate the unity of Arp's oeuvre in its multiplicity.

Arp was doing sculpture even in his early Weggis period (1904–1912). He learned the technique from his friend and colleague Fritz Huf who at that time lived at Lucerne. In the artist's own recollection these sculptures were not unlike his first torsos dating from 1930 and 1931. Unfortunately none of the early sculptures remains in existence, for Arp destroyed all his early work during his Zurich period. Only a few oil paintings, reliefs, and collages, which were kept by his brother or by friends, were rescued from the destructive urge with which Arp was seized after he had hit on his "essential forms," as he put it.

This catalogue of sculptures lists a few transitional forms between relief and sculpture in the round, but others certainly can be found in museums and private collections. So-called Surrealist objects are not included; but I should like to mention, for example, that the Peggy Guggenheim collection in Venice contains a work made of newspapers, entitled *Mutilé et apatride*. Furthermore, I have been unable to locate all those who own sculptures by Arp; therefore I shall be grateful to collectors and museums for any supplementary data and possible indications of omissions and errors.

The catalogue was completed on April 1, 1957. Sales of sculptures or bronze casts made after that date are not listed.

Marguerite Hagenbach

---

1 Shell Profiles. 1930. $26^3/_8 \times 29^7/_8 \times 20^1/_2''$. Wood, private collection, Switzerland. Reproduced p. 44.

2 Hand Fruit. 1930. $21^5/_8 \times 34^5/_8 \times 7^7/_8''$. Wood, private collection, Switzerland. Reproduced p. 45.

3 Gnome, also called Kaspar. 1930. $19^5/_8 \times 11 \times 7^1/_2''$. Plaster, owned by artist. Reproduced p. 54.

4 Head with Annoying Objects. 1930. Face $14^1/_8 \times 10^1/_4 \times 7^1/_2''$, Mustache $5^3/_8 \times 4 \times 3^1/_8''$, Mandolin $5^1/_8 \times 2^3/_8 \times 2''$, Fly $6^1/_4 \times 2^7/_8 \times 4^3/_4''$. Plaster, owned by artist. Reproduced p. 49.

5 Torso. 1930. $12^1/_4 \times 4^3/_4 \times 9^1/_8''$. Plaster original, Claire Goll, Paris; terracotta, Professor H. Hildebrandt, Stuttgart; terracotta, R. Valançay, La Garenne, France; white marble, collection Walter Annenberg, Philadelphia.

6 Figures, One Large and Two Small. 1931. $24^3/_4''$, $17^3/_4''$. Wood, painted white, owned by artist.

7 Bell and Navels. 1931. $10^1/_4''$, $19^1/_4''$. Wood, painted white, owned by artist. Reproduced p. 47.

8 Torso. 1931. $24 \times 16 \times 7^1/_4''$. Base $14^1/_8 \times 10^1/_2 \times 7^1/_8''$. Plaster original, Jürg Spiller, Basel; marble on marble base, collection Müller-Widmann, Basel; bronze (edition of 3): 1, collection M. Lefebvre-Foinet, Paris. Reproduced pp. 86 and 87.

9 Cyprian sculpture. 1931–1938. $6^1/_2 \times 8^5/_8 \times 5''$. White marble, collection François Arp, Paris.

10 To Be Exposed in the Woods (sculpture in three forms). 1932. Large $1^1/_2 \times 8^3/_4 \times 5^1/_2''$; medium $2^3/_4 \times 4^3/_4 \times 3^7/_8''$; small $2 \times 3^5/_8 \times 2^3/_8''$. Plaster original, Paule Vézelay, London; bronze (edition of 5): 1, Paule Vézelay, London; 2, collection Van der Wael, Amsterdam. Reproduced p. 48.

11 To Be Exposed in the Woods (sculpture in two forms). 1932. Large form $2^3/_8 \times 8^3/_8 \times 5''$; small form $1^1/_8 \times 3^5/_8''$. Plaster, owned by artist.

12 Two Thoughts on Navel (sculpture in three forms). 1932. Large form $8^5/_8 \times 8^3/_8 \times 4''$; medium $3^5/_8 \times 2^1/_4 \times 1^3/_4''$; small $2^1/_8 \times ^3/_4 \times 1^1/_2''$. Plaster, owned by artist.

13 Necktie in Silent Tension. 1932. $3^5/_8 \times 3^1/_4 \times 1^3/_4''$. Plaster, owned by artist.

14 Human Concretion. 1933. $22^1/_2 \times 22 \times 13^3/_8''$. Plaster, owned by artist.

15 Shell and Head. 1933. $7^7/_8 \times 9^7/_8 \times 7^1/_4''$. Plaster original, owned by artist; bronze (edition of 5): 1, collection Peggy Guggenheim, Venice; 2, owned by artist.

16 Torso. 1934. $20^7/_8 \times 7^7/_8 \times 10^5/_8''$. Plaster, collection Bruguière, Issy/Paris.

17 Human Concretion. 1934. $13^3/_4 \times 16^1/_2 \times 13^3/_8''$. Plaster original, owned by artist; white marble, private collection, USA.

18 Pagoda Fruit. 1934. $9 \times 13 \times 11''$. Cast cement, owned by artist.

19 Pagoda Fruit on Bowl. 1934. (Derived from No. 18.) Sculpture $9 \times 13 \times 11''$; cup $5^1/_2 \times 15^3/_4 \times 11^3/_8''$. Cast cement, owned by artist.

20 Concrete Sculpture, also called Stone Formed by Human Hand. 1934. $7^7/_8 \times 16^7/_8 \times 8^5/_8''$. White marble, collection Müller-Widmann, Basel.

21 Human Concretion. 1934.
$12^{1}/_{4} \times 22^{7}/_{8} \times 15^{3}/_{4}''$. White marble,
Musée National d'Art Moderne, Paris.

22 Human Concretion on Oval Bowl. 1935.
Sculpture $29^{1}/_{8} \times 18^{1}/_{2} \times 18''$;
bowl $28^{3}/_{8} \times 21 \times 7^{1}/_{2}''$. Limestone,
Kunsthaus, Zurich;
bronze (edition of 3): 1, owned by artist.

23 Human Concretion. 1935.
$28^{3}/_{4} \times 19^{1}/_{4} \times 17^{3}/_{4}''$. Limestone, private
collection, Switzerland; concrete stone,
Museum of Modern Art, New York.
Reproduced pp. 52 and 53.

24 Metamorphosis (Shell-Swan-Swing).
1935. $9 \times 5^{7}/_{8} \times 5^{1}/_{4}''$. Plaster original,
owned by artist; bronze (edition of 5):
1, Mathieu Poncet, St. Germain-en-Laye.

25 Metamorphosis (Shell-Swan-Swing).
1935. (Derived from No. 24.)
$27^{1}/_{8} \times 18^{1}/_{8} \times 16''$. Bronze (edition of 3):
1, collection Graindorge, Liège;
2, patinated black, private collection,
Switzerland; 3, owned by artist.
Reproduced p. 64.

26 Shell Formed by Human Hand. 1935.
$7^{1}/_{2} \times 14 \times 10^{5}/_{8}''$. Pink limestone,
direct cutting*, owned by artist.

27 Angry Fruit. 1936. $14^{1}/_{2} \times 15''$.
Pink limestone, collection G. David
Thompson, Pittsburgh, Pa;
bronze (edition of 3): 1, private
collection, USA.

28 Giant Seed. 1936.
$59 \times 43^{1}/_{4} \times 39^{3}/_{8}''$. Limestone on
revolving base, private collection,
Switzerland. Reproduced p. 50.

29 Lunar Fruit. 1936.
$43^{1}/_{4} \times 59 \times 39^{3}/_{8}''$. Cast cement,
owned by artist.

30 Garland of Buds I. 1936.
$18^{7}/_{8} \times 15 \times 11^{3}/_{8}''$. Pink limestone,
collection Peggy Guggenheim, Venice;
bronze (edition of 3): 1, Kootz Gallery,
New York; 2, patinated black,
collection Mattarazzo, Sao Paulo, Brazil;
concrete stone, Dr. Schwarzmann, Basel.
Reproduced p. 95.

31 Garland of Buds II. 1936.
$20^{1}/_{2} \times 16^{5}/_{8} \times 16^{1}/_{2}''$. Cast cement,
collection Hugnet, Paris.

32 Physiognomic Stone. 1936.
$12^{5}/_{8} \times 17^{3}/_{4} \times 12^{5}/_{8}''$. Plaster original,
owned by artist; pink limestone,
owned by artist.

* Carved directly in the bloc, without preliminary
sketch or plastic model.

33 Concrete Sculpture "Mirr". 1936.
$5^{7}/_{8} \times 6^{3}/_{4} \times 8^{5}/_{8}''$. Bronze (edition of 5):
1, collection M. Hagenbach, Basel;
2, collection Ruth Tillard, Paris;
3, owned by artist.

34 Self-Dissolving Shell. 1936.
$10^{1}/_{4} \times 16^{1}/_{8} \times 8^{5}/_{8}''$. Limestone, direct
cutting, collection Friedrich, Zurich.

35 Marital Sculpture. 1937.
$15^{3}/_{8} \times 11^{1}/_{2} \times 10^{3}/_{4}''$.
Lathe-turned and sawed, executed in
collaboration with Sophie Taeuber-Arp,
owned by artist.

36 Silent Revery. 1937.
$13^{3}/_{8} \times 8^{1}/_{4} \times 5^{7}/_{8}''$; base $6^{7}/_{8}''$, $4^{3}/_{4}''$.
Limestone, direct cutting, on wooden
base, owned by artist; bronze
(edition of 3): 1, on bronze base,
collection Richard K. Weil, St. Louis,
Missouri; 2, on patinated bronze base,
collection S. Kunstadter, Highland Park,
Illinois.

37 Revery. 1937. $14^{5}/_{8} \times 7^{7}/_{8} \times 8^{1}/_{4}''$.
Bronze (edition of 5): 1, owned by artist;
2, Musée d'Art et d'Industrie, St. Etienne.

38 Seated. 1937. $13 \times 15^{3}/_{4} \times 7^{7}/_{8}''$.
Limestone, direct cutting, owned by
artist.

39 Concrete Sculpture with Incisions. 1937.
$13^{3}/_{8} \times 11^{3}/_{8} \times 9^{1}/_{2}''$. Limestone, direct
cutting, collection Friedrich, Zurich.

40 Giant Pip. 1937. $63^{7}/_{8} \times 49^{1}/_{4} \times 30^{1}/_{4}''$.
Limestone, Musée National d'Art
Moderne, Paris.

41 Owl's Dream. 1937/1938.
$10^{1}/_{4} \times 5^{7}/_{8} \times 5^{1}/_{8}''$; base $2^{7}/_{8}$, $5^{1}/_{8}''$.
Limestone on wooden base,
direct cutting, owned by artist. Concrete
stone, collection Gallatin, Philadelphia
Museum of Art, Philadelphia; concrete
stone, collection Michel Seuphor, Paris;
concrete stone, collection M. Lefebvre-
Foinet, Paris; bronze (edition of 3):
1, marble base, Rose Fried Gallery,
New York.

42 Stone Formed by Human Hand.
1937/1938. $16^{1}/_{4} \times 19^{5}/_{8} \times 9^{7}/_{8}''$.
Jura limestone, direct cutting,
Kunstmuseum, Basel (Emanuel Hoffmann
Fund). Reproduced p. 62.

43 Landmark. 1938. $23^{5}/_{8} \times 9^{7}/_{8} \times 14^{1}/_{8}''$.
Wood lathe-turned and sawed, executed
in collaboration with Sophie Taeuber-
Arp, owned by artist.

44 Automatic Sculpture, called The Prisoner.
1938. $10^{5}/_{8} \times 8^{1}/_{4}''$. Black granite, direct
cutting, collection Hendrickz, Brussels.

45 Automatic Sculpture, called Chinese
Shadow Play Figure. 1938.
$7^{1}/_{2} \times 5^{5}/_{8} \times 3^{3}/_{8}''$. Black granite,
direct cutting, collection
R. von Hirsch, Basel.

46 Automatic Sculpture (Homage to Rodin).
1938. $10^{1}/_{4} \times 8^{5}/_{8} \times 4^{1}/_{2}''$. Black granite,
direct cutting, collection
Richard K. Weil, St. Louis,
Missouri.

47 Bud. 1938. $15^{7}/_{8} \times 7^{1}/_{2} \times 7^{7}/_{8}''$.
Plaster, owned by artist.

48 Awakening. 1938. $18^{5}/_{8} \times 9^{1}/_{2} \times 9''$.
Plaster painted green, collection Tunis,
Paris.

49 Growth. 1938. $31^{1}/_{2} \times 9^{7}/_{8} \times 12^{5}/_{8}''$.
White marble, The Solomon Guggen-
heim Museum, New York; bronze
(edition of 3): 1, Philadelphia Museum
of Art, Philadelphia;
2, private collection, USA;
3, collection Mottier, Geneva.
Reproduced p. 63.

50 Lunar Armor. 1938. $12^{5}/_{8} \times 14^{5}/_{8}''$.
Pink limestone, direct cutting,
collection Winston, Birmingham,
Michigan.

51 Pre-Adamic Fruit. 1938.
$11^{1}/_{2} \times 9^{1}/_{8} \times 6^{3}/_{4}''$. Plaster original, owned
by artist; cement, Hugo Weber, Paris;
bronze (edition of 5): 1, Museum of Art,
University of Michigan, Michigan;
2, collection Bally, Montreux.

52 Shell Crystal. 1938.
$10^{5}/_{8} \times 14^{5}/_{8} \times 15''$. Plaster original,
owned by artist; black granite, Nelson
Rockefeller, New York; bronze
(edition of 3): 1, Rijkmuseum Kröller-
Müller, Otterlo; 2, owned by artist.
Reproduced pp. 80 and 81.

53 Column of Building Blocks. 1938.
Sculptural element between two cubes
$16^{7}/_{8}''$, large bowl $5^{1}/_{2}''$, element
consisting of three superimposed bowls
$5^{7}/_{8}''$, block $3^{1}/_{8} \times 5^{1}/_{8} \times 5^{1}/_{8}''$. Plaster,
owned by artist.

54 Pre-Adamic Torso. 1938.
$18^{7}/_{8} \times 12^{5}/_{8} \times 13^{3}/_{4}''$. Pink limestone,
collection M. Hagenbach, Basel;
bronze (edition of 3): 1, Kootz Gallery,
New York; 2, owned by artist.

55 Shell. 1938. $4^{3}/_{4} \times 4^{3}/_{4} \times 3^{7}/_{8}''$.
Bronze (edition of 5): 1, Jane Wade,
New York; 2, collection
G. David Thompson, Pittsburgh;
3, collection Herwin Schaefer, Berkeley,
California; stainless steel, owned by
artist.

56 Shell. 1938. (Derived from No. 55.)
9 × 11 × 8¹/₄″. Black granite,
collection Mrs. Culver Orswell,
Pomfret Center, Connecticut, USA;
bronze (edition of 3): 1, collection
Kunstadter, Highland Park, Illinois;
2, collection Van der Wael, Amsterdam;
3, collection Judge and Mrs. Henri
Epstein, New York. Reproduced p. 66.

57 Small Leaning Figure, called Egyptian
Woman. 1938.
10¹/₄ × 9 × 4³/₄″. Bronze (edition of 5):
1, collection M. Hagenbach, Basel;
2, collection J. Lazard, Paris;
3, Will Grohmann, Berlin;
4, Sidney Janis Gallery, New York;
5, owned by artist.

58 Crystal. 1938/1939. 2⁷/₈ × 3⁷/₈ × 4¹/₂″.
Painted plaster (original), collection
Bruguière, Issy/Paris; bronze (edition
of 3): 1, collection Ruth Tillard, Paris.

59 Crystal in a Cup. 1939.
9¹/₂ × 13³/₄ × 11³/₈″. Plaster, owned by
artist.

60 Lingam. 1939. 6³/₈ × 5¹/₈ × 4⁷/₈″.
Bronze (edition of 5): 1, collection
Ruth Tillard, Paris; 2, collection
M. Hagenbach, Basel; 3, collection Judy
and Kenneth Arenberg, Highland Park,
Illinois; 4, collection Beer de Turig,
Paris; 5, owned by artist.

61 Star. 1939. 4⁵/₈ × 6³/₈ × 1³/₄″.
Base 5¹/₈, 4³/₈″. Plaster original,
collection Virgil Thompson, New York;
bronze (edition of 5): 1, private collection,
USA; 2, private collection, USA;
3, lead, private collection, USA;
4, private collection, Switzerland;
5, on bronze base, Baroness Lambert,
Brussels. Reproduced p. 94.

62 Pyramid Leaf. 1939. 9¹/₂″. Black granite,
collection Senior Jr., New York.

63 Leaf. 1941. 16⁷/₈ × 9⁵/₈ × 9⁵/₈″. White
marble, collection Friedrich, Zurich.
Reproduced p. 68.

64 Dream Amphora. 1941. 9⁵/₈ × 9 × 5¹/₄″.
Plaster original, collection Friedrich,
Zurich; white marble, collection Bayer,
Aspen, Colorado; white marble,
collection Richard K. Weil, St. Louis,
Missouri; bronze (edition of 3):
1, owned by artist.

65 Mediterranean Sculpture I, also called
Orphic Dream. 1941. 15 × 10⁵/₈ × 6³/₈″.
White marble, private collection, USA;
terracotta, owned by artist; bronze
(edition of 3): 1, Nelly van Doesburg,
Meudon; 2, owned by artist.
Reproduced pp. 70 and 71.

66 Mediterranean Group. 1941/1942.
8¹/₄ × 11⁷/₈ × 2⁷/₈″. Bronze (edition of 5):
1, Max Ernst, Sedona, USA;
2, Gerd Hatje, Stuttgart;
3, Galerie Denise René, Paris.
Reproduced p. 69.

67 Mediterranean Sculpture II. 1942.
15 × 10⁵/₈ × 6³/₈″. White marble,
private collection, USA;
Cristallino marble, owned by artist.

68 Pagan Stone. 1942. 5⁷/₈ × 10¹/₂ × 4³/₄″.
Plaster original, owned by artist; black
granite, collection Meric Callery,
New York.
Reproduced p. 65.

69 Concrete Form from Two Realms. 1942.
14¹/₈ × 5¹/₂ × 5¹/₂″. Plaster original,
Ruth Tillard, Paris; white marble,
collection Boesiger, Zurich; white marble,
private collection, USA; white marble,
private collection, Italy.
Reproduced p. 75.

70 Little Sphinx. 1942. 7¹/₂ × 16¹/₈ × 4³/₈″
(without base). Bronze (edition of 5):
1, patinated green, private collection,
USA; 2, patinated black with base,
Galerie Drouin, Paris.
Reproduced p. 56.

71 Siren. 1942. 17³/₄ × 13³/₈ × 9¹/₈″.
Bronze (edition of 5): 1, collection
G. David Thompson, Pittsburgh;
2, Sidney Janis Gallery, New York;
3, owned by artist.
Reproduced p. 57.

72 Alu with Claws. 1942. 22¹/₈ × 15¹/₂ × 11¹/₂″.
Bronze (edition of 5): 1, Galleria
Internazionale d'Arte Moderna, Venice;
2, Sidney Janis Gallery, New York;
3, Gerald Cramer, Geneva;
4, owned by artist.

73 Somersault. 1942. 13⁷/₈ × 12³/₄ × 10¹/₄″.
Bronze (edition of 5): 1, Galerie Drouin,
Paris; 2, Sidney Janis Gallery, New York;
3, Henry Kleeman, Munich-New York;
4, owned by artist.

74 Silent Sculpture "Corneille". 1942.
11 × 12³/₈ × 10¹/₄″. Plaster, owned by
artist.

75 Silent Sculpture "Corneille". 1942.
(Derived from No. 74.)
19⁵/₈ × 21⁵/₈ × 17³/₄″. Limestone,
Galleria d'Arte Moderna, Turin;
limestone, collection J. Lazard, Paris.

76 Geometric-Ageometric. 1942.
11³/₈ × 11¹/₈ × 6³/₈″. Bronze (edition of 5):
1, collection Magnelli, Paris; 2, collection
Friedrich, Zurich; 3, owned by artist.
Reproduced p. 78.

77 Form Heard and Seen. 1942.
13³/₈ × 7¹/₄ × 6⁷/₈″. Plaster original,
owned by artist; marble, collection
M. Hagenbach, Basel; bronze
(edition of 5): 1, owned by artist.

78 Dream Figure. 1942. 12¹/₄ × 7¹/₈ × 3⁷/₈″
(without base); base 5⁷/₈, 3⁷/₈″. White
marble on steel base, private collection,
USA; white marble on steel base,
collection Petzold, Basel.

79 Snake Bread. 1942. 6¹/₄ × 10¹/₄ × 6¹/₄″.
Plaster original, owned by artist;
black granite, private collection, USA.
Reproduced p. 65.

80 Silent. 1942. 13³/₈ × 5¹/₂ × 4³/₈″.
Plaster original, owned by artist; white
marble, Mrs. John D. Rockefeller III,
New York; white marble, collection
Petzold, Basel. Reproduced p. 74.

81 Silent Sculpture. 1942. 13³/₄ × 7¹/₈″.
White marble, collection Edgar Kauf-
mann Jr., New York.

82 Automatic Sculpture, called Chinese
Shadow Play Figure. 1947. (Derived
from No. 45). Pink limestone, Michel
Seuphor, Paris; bronze (edition of 3):
1, owned by artist.

83 Human Concretion on Oval Bowl. 1947.
(Derived from No. 21).
Sculpture 12¹/₄ × 22⁷/₈ × 15³/₄″; bowl
⁵/₈ × 23¹/₄ × 16⁷/₈″. Bronze (edition of 3):
1, owned by artist.

84 Dream Animal. 1947. 15³/₈ × 8 × 7⁷/₈″.
Plaster original, owned by artist; bronze
(edition of 5): 1, Kootz Gallery, New
York; 2, patinated green, private
collection, Switzerland; 3, private
collection, Brussels; 4, Sidney Janis
Gallery, New York; 5, Galerie d'Art
Moderne, Basel.

85 Bird Skeleton. 1947. 15³/₄ × 8⁵/₈ × 7¹/₈″.
Bronze (edition of 5): 1, collection
F. C. Graindorge, Liège; 2, owned by
artist.

86 Cup with Small Chimera. 1947.
31¹/₂ × 17³/₈ × 12⁵/₈″. Plaster original,
owned by artist; bronze (edition of 3):
1, collection Mrs. Warren, New York;
2, patinated black, Galleria Nazionale
d'Arte Moderna, Rome; 3, owned by
artist. Reproduced p. 59.

87 Tree of Bowls. 1947. 39³/₈ × 19⁵/₈″.
Bronze (edition of 3): 1, Openlucht-
museum voor Beeldhouwkunst,
Middelheim-Antwerp;
2, patinated black, collection
Richard K. Weil, St. Louis, Missouri.
Reproduced pp. 82 and 83.

88 Necktie in Silent Tension. 1947.
(Derived from No. 13.)
$5^5/_8 \times 11^7/_8 \times 8^5/_8''$. Black granite,
private collection, USA.

89 Human Concretion on Oval Bowl. 1948.
(Derived from No. 23.) Sculpture
$28^3/_4 \times 19^3/_8 \times 17^3/_4''$; cup
$7^1/_2 \times 28^3/_8 \times 21''$. Bronze (edition of 3):
1, owned by artist.

90 Head with Claws. 1949. $18^1/_2 \times 9 \times 7^1/_2''$.
Plaster original, owned by artist; bronze
(edition of 5): 1, private collection, USA.
Reproduced p. 58.

91 Gnome Form. 1949. $15^3/_8 \times 5^7/_8 \times 7^1/_8''$.
White marble, collection Friedrich,
Zurich; bronze (edition of 5): 1, Galerie
Denise René, Paris.

92 Bust of Gnome. 1949. $12^3/_8 \times 5^5/_8 \times 3^7/_8''$.
Plaster original, owned by artist; marble,
collection George Bortin, Philadelphia;
bronze (edition of 5): 1, private collection,
USA; 2, Galerie Denise René, Paris;
3, owned by artist. Reproduced p. 55.

93 From Gnomeland. 1949. $9^7/_8 \times 8 \times 3^7/_8''$.
Plaster original, owned by artist; white
marble, collection G. David Thompson,
Pittsburgh; bronze (edition of 5):
1, collection Hans Richter, Southbury,
Connecticut; 2, collection Arcay, Vélizy,
Paris; 3, private collection, USA;
4, Galerie d'Art Moderne, Basel.
Reproduced p. 60.

94 Mythical Sculpture. 1949.
$11^7/_8 \times 5^5/_8 \times 4^3/_8''$. Bronze (edition of 5):
1, collection Ströher, Darmstadt;
2, owned by artist.

95 Mythical Figure. 1949.
$25^1/_2 \times 11^7/_8 \times 10^5/_8''$. (Derived from
No. 94.) Limestone, collection G. David
Thompson, Pittsburgh; concrete stone,
owned by artist.

96 Gargoyle. 1949. $11^1/_2 \times 9 \times 5^7/_8''$.
Limestone, direct cutting, owned by
artist.

97 Pagoda Fruit. 1949. (Derived from
No. 18). $55^1/_8 \times 27^5/_8 \times 25^5/_8''$. Bronze
(edition of 3): 1, patinated black, Tate
Gallery, London; 2, owned by artist.
Reproduced p. 51.

98 Concrete Sculpture "Mirr". 1949/1950.
(Derived from No. 33.) $13 \times 14^5/_8 \times 19''$.
Black granite, collection Herbert Roth-
schild, New York and Kichewan, N.Y.;
bronze (edition of 3): 1, owned by artist.

99 Silent. 1949. (Derived from No. 80.)
$24 \times 9^7/_8 \times 7^7/_8''$ (without base). White
marble, steel and granite base, collection
J. Rosen, Baltimore.

100 Human Lunar Spectral. 1950.
$11 \times 8^3/_4 \times 6^3/_4''$. Limestone, direct
cutting, owned by artist; bronze
(edition of 5): 1, privately owned,
England; plaster, privately owned,
Brazil; plaster, privately owned, Paris.

101 Human Lunar Spectral. 1950.
(Derived from No. 100.)
$32^5/_8 \times 25^5/_8 \times 19^5/_8''$. Pink limestone,
Museo d'Arte Moderna, Rio de Janeiro;
white marble on base ($36^5/_8 \times 25^5/_8 \times 19^5/_8$),
collection Dotremont, Brussels; bronze
(edition of 3): 1, collection Elisabeth
Müller, Basel-Hollywood; concrete
stone, owned by artist.
Reproduced pp. 90 and 91.

102 Lunar Cavernous Spectral. 1950.
$16^1/_2 \times 7^7/_8 \times 6''$. Limestone, direct
cutting, owned by artist; white marble,
collection Sprengel, Hannover.

103 Idol. 1950. $42^7/_8 \times 15 \times 8^1/_4''$. Plaster
original, owned by artist; plaster cast,
collection Giedion-Welcker, Zurich;
bronze (edition of 3): 1, collection
Urvater, Brussels; 2, collection Baroness
Lambert, Brussels.
Reproduced p. 89.

104 Mythical Figure. 1950.
$44^1/_2 \times 15^1/_8 \times 13^3/_4''$. Plaster original,
collection Zervos, Paris.

105 Small Mythical Figure. 1950.
$28 \times 6^3/_8 \times 6^7/_8''$. Plaster original, owned
by artist.
Reproduced p. 88.

106 Small Mythical Figure. 1950.
$37^3/_4 \times 6^1/_4 \times 6^7/_8''$. Plaster original,
owned by artist.

107 Pistil. 1950. $13^3/_8 \times 6^3/_4 \times 4^7/_8''$.
Limestone, direct cutting, owned by
artist.

108 Pistil. 1950. (Derived from No. 107.)
$34^5/_8 \times 15^3/_4 \times 14^1/_8''$. Pink limestone,
private collection, USA.

109 Snake Movement I. 1950.
$8^1/_4 \times 13^3/_8 \times 11^3/_8''$. White marble,
private collection, USA.
Reproduced p. 84.

110 Sling. 1950. $11^3/_4 \times 8 \times 6^7/_8''$. Limestone,
direct cutting, owned by artist.

111 Pagan Fruit. 1950. (Derived from No. 68.)
$11^1/_2 \times 21^1/_4 \times 9^1/_8''$. Wood, owned by
artist.

112 Cyprian Sculpture. 1951. (Derived from
No. 9.) $15^3/_4 \times 22^5/_8 \times 12^3/_4''$. White
marble, private collection, USA.
Reproduced p. 67.

113 Owl's Dream. 1951. (Derived from
No. 41.) $15^3/_4 \times 9 \times 7^7/_8''$. Marble,
collection Lee Ault, New Canaan, USA;
steel (edition of 3): 1, collection
G. David Thompson, Pittsburgh;
2, collection Bally, Montreux;
3, Mrs. Florsheim, Chicago.
Reproduced pp. 72 and 73.

114 Hurlou. 1951. $19^5/_8 \times 7^1/_2 \times 8^1/_4''$. Pink
limestone, Ralph F. Collin, New York;
bronze (edition of 5): 1, Sidney Janis
Gallery, New York; 2, Galerie Denise
René, Paris.

115 Amphora Fruit. 1951. $39^3/_8 \times 21^5/_8''$.
Plaster original, owned by artist; bronze
(edition of 3): 1, collection Peggy
Guggenheim, Venice.

116 Thales of Miletus. 1951.
$41^3/_4 \times 9 \times 10''$. Black granite,
collection G. David Thompson,
Pittsburgh.

117 Mythical Wineskin. 1952.
$13^3/_4 \times 19^5/_8 \times 17^3/_8''$. Plaster original,
owned by artist; pink limestone, Art
Institute of Chicago; bronze (edition of
3): 1, owned by artist.

118 Cobra-Centaur. 1952. $30^3/_4 \times 16^7/_8 \times 9''$.
Plaster original, owned by artist; white
marble, Kunstmuseum, Winterthur;
bronze (edition of 3): 1, patinated black,
collection von Hirsch, Basel;
2, collection Neumann, Chicago,
Illinois; 3, Art Institute of Chicago,
Chicago, Illinois.

119 Bud. 1952. (Derived from No. 47.)
$37 \times 17^3/_8 \times 18^1/_4''$. Cristallino marble,
family vault Prof. Schwarz, central
cemetery, Basel.

120 Torso. 1953. (Derived from No. 5.)
$34^5/_8 \times 13^3/_8 \times 10^5/_8''$. White marble,
Museum of Smith College, North
Hampton, Mass.

121 Torso. 1953. (Derived from No. 5.)
$34^5/_8 \times 13^3/_8 \times 10^5/_8''$. White marble,
Wallraf Richartz Museum, Cologne.

122 Shepherd of Clouds. 1953. (Derived from
No. 91.) $10'6'' \times 48^3/_8'' \times 7'2^5/_8''$. Plaster
original, destroyed; bronze,
Ciudad Universitaria, Caracas, Venezuela.
Reproduced p. 61.

123 Shepherd of Clouds. 1953.
(Derived from No. 91.) $63 \times 24 \times 29^1/_8''$.
Bronze, owned by artist.

124 Silent. 1953. $47^1/_4 \times 17^3/_4 \times 18^1/_2''$.
Plaster original, owned by artist; bronze
(edition of 3): 1, patinated black,
collection Carlos Raul Villanueva,
Caracas, Venezuela.

125 Oru. 1953. $8^5/_8 \times 11^3/_4 \times 15^3/_4''$. Plaster original, owned by artist; concrete stone, private collection, Milan; white marble, collection G. David Thompson, Pittsburgh. Reproduced p. 79.

126 Aquatic. 1953. $9^1/_2 \times 13^3/_4 \times 25^1/_2''$. Plaster original, owned by artist; white marble, Walker Art Center, Minneapolis, Minnesota.

127 Relative. $9 \times 3^1/_8 \times 3^1/_2''$. Wood, collection M. Hagenbach, Basel.

128 Ptolemy. 1953. $40^1/_2 \times 20^7/_8 \times 16^7/_8''$. Limestone (Euville), collection Burden, New York; bronze (edition of 3): 1, collection Dr. Peter Nathan, Zurich. Reproduced pp. 96 and 97.

129 Leaf on Crystal. 1954. $17^7/_8 \times 9^1/_2 \times 8^5/_8''$. Plaster original, owned by artist; white marble, collection Van der Wael, Amsterdam. Reproduced pp. 76 and 77.

130 Baptismal Font. 1954. Marble, white metal lid, All Saints' Church, Basel.

131 From the Land of Thales. 1954. $8^1/_4 \times 15 \times 10^1/_4''$. Plaster original, owned by artist; bronze (edition of 5): 1, owned by artist; 2, owned by artist.

132 Ganymed. 1954. $8^1/_4 \times 13 \times 10^1/_4''$. Terracotta, collection Ströher, Darmstadt; terracotta, owned by artist.

133 Dream Flower with Lips. 1954. $18^1/_8 \times 6 \times 3^7/_8''$. Plaster, owned by artist.

134 Dream Flower with Lips. 1954. (Derived from No. 133.) $31^1/_2 \times 10^5/_8 \times 6^7/_8''$. Marble on marble base, Mrs. H. Gates Lloyd, Washington, D.C.

135 Snake Movement II. 1955. $8^1/_4 \times 13^3/_8 \times 11^3/_8''$. Limestone, taille directe, owned by artist; bronze (edition of 3): 1, collection Arenberg, Chicago: 2, owned by artist.

136 Snake Movement II. 1955. (Derived from No. 135.) $17^3/_8 \times 29^1/_8 \times 22^7/_8''$. Limestone (Lens), owned by artist; yellow concrete stone, collection Witzig, Güttingen, Switzerland; white concrete stone, collection Nelson Rockefeller, New York. Reproduced p. 85.

137 Structural Column (three forms). 1955. (Derived from No. 53.) $64^7/_8''$. Forms I and II (structural elements) $24 \times 8^5/_8 \times 7^7/_8''$, Form III (three bowls superimposed) $17^3/_8 \times 7^1/_2 \times 7^1/_2''$. Bronze (edition of 3): 1, owned by artist.

138 Daphne. 1955. $48 \times 14^1/_8 \times 11^3/_4''$. Bronze, collection Frigerio, Paris. Reproduced pp. 92 and 93.

139 Sleep. 1955. $6^1/_4 \times 11^7/_8 \times 6^3/_4''$. Limestone, direct cutting, owned by artist.

140 Anguishing Configuration. 1955. $11^3/_4 \times 7^1/_4 \times 5^1/_2''$. Limestone, direct cutting, owned by artist.

141 Outline of a Life. 1955. $40^1/_2 \times 16^1/_2 \times 10^5/_8''$. Plaster, owned by artist.

142 Mediterranean Sculpture II. 1956. (Derived from No. 67.) $24^3/_8 \times 17^3/_8 \times 10^5/_8''$. Cristallino marble, owned by artist.

143 Star. 1956. (Derived from No. 61.) $16^3/_8 \times 13 \times 2^1/_2''$, base $8^5/_8''$, $6^3/_4''$. Bronze (edition of 3): 1, collection Bally, Montreux.

144 Self-Absorbed. 1956. $21^5/_8 \times 9^7/_8 \times 7^7/_8''$. Limestone, direct cutting, owned by artist.

145 Venus of Meudon. 1956. $62^1/_4 \times 15^3/_4 \times 15^3/_4''$ (without base), base $13^3/_4''$, $15^3/_4''$. Plaster, owned by artist.

146 Domestic Object. 1956. $14^1/_8 \times 6^1/_4 \times 9^7/_8''$. Plaster, owned by artist.

147 Nameless. 1957. $19^5/_8 \times 7^1/_8 \times 4^3/_4''$. Plaster original, owned by artist; bronze (edition of 5): 1, owned by artist.

Bibliography

This bibliography makes no claim to completeness. It is based on the bibliography prepared in 1947 by Bernard Karpel, librarian of the Museum of Modern Art in New York, for Arp's *On My Way,* in close collaboration with the artist and myself, which I have brought up to date. Moreover, I have rearranged the first two sections so that they are now in chronological order. Arp's poems, essays, original graphic works, and illustrations are combined into a single listing to avoid cross-references, and the section "Collective Statements" is entirely omitted. The section "Writings on Arp" is arranged alphabetically by authors, and chronologically within each entry. The exhibition catalogues are listed under the names of the galleries; catalogues containing original texts or graphic works by Arp are also listed in Section B (such items are cross-referenced). The titles of books, poems, essays, periodicals, etc. are given in each case in the language in which they were published.

I ask the reader's indulgence for unintentional omissions and errors. I leave the making of an exhaustive list of Arp's poetic works in German and in French, and of his extensive graphic productions to professional bibliographers. My own contribution is intended merely as an incentive and a guide to them.

Meudon, July 1, 1957   Marguerite Hagenbach

A. Books and Portfolios of Graphic Works by Jean Arp

1 hans arp 8 bois. 10 pp., Constance, 1920. *Original woodcuts, edited and prefaced by Otto Flake.*

2 der vogel selbdritt. 32 pp., privately printed (by Otto v. Holten), Berlin, 1920. *Poems, 6 original woodcuts. First publication of poems of the Dada period. 150 numbered copies.*

3 die wolkenpumpe. 22 pp., Die Silbergäule, v. 50/51. Paul Steegemann Verlag, Hannover, 1920. *Poems of the Dada period. Drawing on cover by Arp.*

4 7 Arpaden. Merz 5, Arp-Mappe, Hannover, n. d. (1923?) Second portfolio of the Merz publishing house. *7 original lithographs, title page by Schwitters. 50 numbered copies.*

5 Der Pyramidenrock. 70 pp., Eugen Rentsch Verlag, Erlenbach-Zurich and Munich, n. d. (1924). *Poems of the Dada period. Portrait of Arp (drawing) by Amedeo Modigliani.*

6 Gedichte. – Weisst du schwarzt du. 32 pp., pra-Verlag (privately printed), Zurich, 1930. *5 collages by Max Ernst. Poems 1922, collages 1929.*

7 Konfiguration. 10 pp., Poésie & Co., Paris, 1930. *Poems. Drawing on cover by Arp.*

8 Tres inmensas novelas (Tres novelas ejemplares). (By Arp and Vicente Huidobro). 84 pp., Editorial Zig-Zag, Santiago, 1935. *Portrait of Arp by Modigliani, portrait of Huidobro by Arp, drawing on cover by Huidobro from a drawing by Arp. Composed jointly in French by Arp and Huidobro, Spanish version by Huidobro. Written at Arcachon in 1931.*

9 Des taches dans le vide. 6 pp., Les feuillets de Sagesse, collection anthologique, No. 32. Librairie Tschann, Paris, 1937. *Poems.*

10 Sciure de gamme. 12 pp., Collection Un Divertissement. Parisot, Paris, 1938. *Poems.*

11 Muscheln und Schirme. 36 pp., privately printed, Meudon-Val-Fleury, 1939. *Poems. Drawing by Sophie Taeuber. Typography by Jan Tschichold.*

12 Poèmes sans prénoms. 36 pp., privately printed, Grasse, 1941. *Poems. Cover and 3 drawings by Sophie Taeuber-Arp. 150 numbered copies, of which 10 (Nos. 1–10) contain a color drawing by Sophie Taeuber-Arp.*

13 Rire de coquille. 12 pp., Vordemberge-Gildewart, Amsterdam, 1944. *Poems. 4 drawings by Sophie Taeuber-Arp. 100 numbered copies, dedicated to Sophie Taeuber-Arp. 25 copies on Barchem green, 75 on Van Gelder Holland paper.*

14 1924–1925–1926–1943: Gedichte. 25 pp., Benteli, Bern-Bümpliz, 1944. *Drawing by Sophie Taeuber-Arp, December 1942. Typography by Jan Tschichold. 250 copies.*

15 Le Blanc aux pieds de nègre. 30 pp., Collection l'Age d'Or, No. 11. Edition de la revue Fontaine, Paris, 1945. *Poems in prose. 25 numbered copies (I–XXV) on vergé d'arches, 400 (1–400) on vélin.*

16 11 configurations. Allianz-Verlag, Zurich, 1945. *11 original woodcuts, ed. and introd. by Max Bill. Text by Gabrielle Buffet-Picabia. 20 numbered copies (I–XX) boxed with signed reproduction of woodblock, 40 copies (1–40) with additional woodcut, signed, 160 copies (41–200).*

17 Le Siège de l'air. Poèmes 1915–1945. 140 pp., Vrille, Paris, 1946. *Poems, 8 double drawings by Arp and Sophie Taeuber-Arp. Preface by Alain Gheerbrant, cover by Arp. 30 copies on vélin with an original woodcut in two prints on China and Japan and an original torn paper, 70 copies with a graphic work by Arp, 900 copies on white vélin.*

18 Trois nouvelles exemplaires (by Arp and Vicente Huidobro). 51 pp., Collection l'Age d'Or, No. 20. Edition de la revue Fontaine, Paris, 1946. *Translated from the Spanish by Rilka Walter. Cf. No. 8.*

19 On My Way – Poetry and Essays 1912–1947. 148 pp., The Documents of Modern Art. Wittenborn, Schultz, Inc., New York, 1948. *Poems and essays. Original texts in German and in French, translated into English by Ralph Manheim. Preface by Robert Motherwell. Essay by Carola Giedion-*

Welcker, translated by A. E. van Eyck. Biographical notes by Gabrielle Buffet-Picabia. Bibliography by Bernard Karpel. 2 original woodcuts, 48 reproductions.

20 Onze peintres vus par Arp. Taeuber Kandinsky Leuppi Vordemberge Arp Delaunay Schwitters Kiesler Morris Magnelli Ernst. 44 pp., Edition Girsberger, Zurich, 1949. Edition of 1,500 copies, of which 200 are numbered and contain 3 original woodcuts by Arp, Kandinsky, and Leuppi.

21 Elemente. Holzschnitte. Entwürfe aus dem Jahre 1920. Second Stubendruck, Zurich, 1950. 10 woodcuts, carved and printed by hand by Karl Schmid, 1949. Poem by Arp, "Ich träumte von den vier Elementen". Typography by Alfred Willimann. 200 copies, numbered and signed.

22 Souffle. 12 pp., Editions PAB, Alès, 1950. Poem. Woodcut of 1918. 50 copies printed by P. A. Benoît for New Year's 1950.

23 Auch das ist nur eine Wolke. Aus den Jahren 1920–1950. 82 pp., Vineta-Verlag, Basel, 1951. Poems in prose. 4 slightly reduced reproductions of cut-outs by Jean Arp,

colored by artist. Preface by A. M. Frey. 130 numbered and signed copies.

24 Wegweiser – Jalons. 24 pp., privately printed, 1951. Prose, bilingual. German text translated into French by Robert Valançay and Arp. 3 reproductions. Typography by Jan Tschichold. Edition of 250 numbered copies on handmade paper.

25 Dreams and Projects. Curt Valentin, New York, 1951/1952. Poems translated into English by Ralph Manheim. 28 original woodcuts. Original texts in German and in French: Zwischen den Zeilen der Zeit, Nun sind die Euter verdorrt, In die strahlende Stille, Fragt man die Flügel, Schatten. Edition of 320 copies, of which 25 (1–25) with additional set of woodcuts on Japan paper.

26 Die Engelsschrift. Privately printed (by H. Laupp jr. at Tübingen), 1952. Poem. Lithograph by Sophie Taeuber-Arp and Hans Arp. Typography by Jan Tschichold. Edition of 110 copies.

27 Wortträume und schwarze Sterne. Auswahl aus den Gedichten der Jahre 1911–1952. 96 pp., Limes-Verlag, Wiesbaden,

1953. Poems. 4 reproductions. Preface: Wegweiser. Cover by Arp. Special edition of 100 numbered copies on handmade paper with 4 original woodcuts, signed.

28 Behaarte Herzen 1923–1926, Könige vor der Sintflut 1952–1953. 52 pp., Meta-Verlag, Frankfurt a. M., 1953. Poems. Short bibliography and biography. 100 numbered copies with the original woodcut "Fish" for frontispiece and signed woodcut "Shell Face".

29 Auf einem Bein. 32 pp., Dichtung unserer Zeit, fasc. 1. Limes-Verlag, Wiesbaden, 1955. Poems. Drawing on cover by Arp.

30 ARP collages. 24 pp., Berggruen & Cie., Paris, 1955. Text, cover (photo déchirée) by Arp. 18 color plates.

31 Unsern täglichen Traum ... Erinnerungen, Dichtungen und Betrachtungen aus den Jahren 1914–1954. 128 pp., Im Verlag der Arche, Zurich, 1955. Dust cover by Arp. 14 reproductions. Biographical data and bibliography by Hans Bolliger.

32 Worte mit und ohne Anker. Limes-Verlag, Wiesbaden, announced for 1957. Cover, drawings by Arp.

B. Poems, Prose and Illustrations by Jean Arp

33 Moderner Bund, Zweite Ausstellung. Kunsthaus Zurich, fasc. 1, Zurich, 1912. Woodcut, 6 initials and vignettes by Arp. Edition of 200 copies, of which 50 numbered.

34 Der blaue Reiter, ed. W. Kandinsky and F. Marc. R. Piper & Co., Munich, 1912. Initials by Arp, and a reproduction of one of his works. Pp. 69, 74, 103, 105.

35 Arp, Hans. Von der letzten Malerei. Der Sturm 4, No. 188/189, December 1913, Berlin. Poetic notes.

36 Arp, Hans. Von Zeichnungen aus der Kokoschka-Mappe. Der Sturm 4, No. 190/191, December 1913, Berlin, p. 151. Poetic notes.

37 Bhagavad-Gita. Le chant du bienheureux. Edition de la Librairie de l'art indépendant, St. Armand, Cher, n. d. (1914?). 12 illustrations from pen drawings by Arp.

38 Galerie Tanner. Moderne Wandteppiche, Stickereien, Malereien, Zeichnungen. Zurich, 1915. Cover by Arp.

39 Sirius, No. 2, 1915/1916, Zurich. Drawing by Arp: Crucifixion.

40 Cabaret Voltaire. Eine Sammlung künstlerischer und literarischer Beiträge. Ed.

Hugo Ball, Zurich, 1916. Drawing on cover and 2 illustrations by Arp. Portrait of Arp by Modigliani.

41 Huelsenbeck, Richard. Phantastische Gebete. Collection Dada, Zurich, 1916. 7 woodcuts by Arp.

42 Huelsenbeck, Richard. Schalaben, schalabai, schalamezomai. Collection Dada, Zurich, 1916. 4 drawings by Arp.

43 Dada 1. Zurich, July 1917. 2 original woodcuts by Arp.

44 Dada 3 (German edition). Zurich, December 7, 1918. 8 original woodcuts by Arp. (The French edition of Dada 3 contains only 5 original woodcuts by Arp.)

45 Kunstsalon Wolfsberg. Die neue Kunst. Zurich, 1918. Catalogue of exhibition. 2 original woodcuts by Arp. Cf. No. 293.

46 Tzara, Tristan. Vingt cinq poèmes. Collection Dada, Zurich, 1918. Drawing on cover and 10 woodcuts by Arp. Special edition of 10 numbered copies on Holland paper, signed by author and Arp.

46a Arp, Hans. (Poems.) In: Der Zeltweg. Zurich, Verlag Mouvement Dada, 1919. Die Hyperbel vom Krokodil-Coiffeur und dem Spa-

zierstock, written in collaboration with Serner and Tzara. Other poems from: die wolkenpumpe. Cover and woodcut by Arp.

47 Arp, Hans. (Poems.) Anthologie Dada (Dada 4/5), Zurich, 5. 15. 1919. Cover (original woodcut) and 4 further original woodcuts by Arp. (The French edition of Dada 4/5 contains 5 woodcuts but no poems by Arp.)

48 Arp, Hans. De "La pompe des nuages". De "Perroquet supérieur". Littérature 2, No. 14, Paris, June 1920. Translated from the German by André Breton and Tristan Tzara.

49 Arp, Hans. Gedichte aus dem "cacadou supérieur". In: Die Schammade, Dadameter (Dilettanten erhebt euch). Cologne, Schloemilch-Verlag, 1920. Cover (original woodcut), 3 reproductions of works by Arp. A few de luxe copies.

50 Arp, Hans. Die Schwalbenhode. Dada-Almanach, im Auftrage des Zentralamts der deutschen Dada-Bewegung hrsg. von Richard Huelsenbeck. Pp. 114–116, 145–146. Erich Reiss-Verlag, Berlin, 1920. Poems. (Later most of them were published under the title der vogel selbdritt.)

51 Manifeste du Crocodarium Dada. Littérature 2, No. 13, Paris, May 1920. *Written by Tristan Tzara, but signed with Arp's name.*

52 Tzara, Tristan. Cinéma calendrier du coeur abstrait. Maisons. Collection Dada, en dépôt au Sans Pareil, Paris, 1920. *19 woodcuts by Arp. Edition of 150 numbered copies. Cuts destroyed.*

53 Arp, Hans. Die Schwalbenhode, No. 4. Der anfang des fadens bei diesem knäuel. Déclaration. s'Fatagagalied (with Max Ernst). In: Dada Au Grandair – Der Sängerkrieg INtirol, Tarrenz b. Imst, 16. Sept. 1886–1921, en dépôt au Sans Pareil, Paris, 1921.

54 Péret, Benjamin. Le passager du transatlantique. Collection Dada, Au Sans Pareil, Paris, n. d. (1921?). *4 drawings by Arp. 50 copies, 3 on China paper.*

55 MA Aktivista Folyoirat, Vienna, 3. 15. 1922. *2 original woodcuts and cover by Arp*

56 Arp, Hans. Die Hasenkaserne. Merz, No. 4. Hannover, July 1923.

57 Arp, Hans. Arabische Sprichwörter. Das bezungte Brett. Die Etablierung der Eulalia. Merz 6 (Arp 1), Hannover, October 1923.

58 Arp, Hans. Wee onze goede Kaspar is dood. Mecano, No. 4/5. Ed. Van Doesburg, Leiden, 1923. *Translated from the German into Dutch by Th. van Doesburg.*

59 Arp, Hans. Befiederte Steine. Der Sturm 14, No. 11, Berlin, 1923, pp. 165–167. *4 poems.*

60 Arp, Hans and Kurt Schwitters. Der Würfel. Der Sturm 14, No. 12, Berlin, 1923. Pp. 184, 186.

61 Tzara, Tristan. De nos oiseaux: poèmes. Editions des Feuilles Libres et Editions Kra, Paris, 1923. *10 drawings by Arp. Also a special edition of 20 signed copies, 10 on Japan and 10 on Holland paper.*

62 Arp, Hans. Devant la chambre les fileuses les lions. The Little Review, London, Spring 1924, p. 22. *Poems.*

63 Arp, Hans. Das bezungte Brett. Der poussierte Gast. Sekundenzeiger. G (periodical), June 1924, Berlin, pp. 48/49. *Poems from the volume Einzahl, Mehrzahl, Rübezahl (Published as Der Pyramidenrock, cf. No. 5). 7 reduced drawings from the Arp portfolio of the Merz-Verlag, Hannover. Portrait (photo).*

64 Arp, Hans. Die Blumensphinx. Das lichtscheue Paradies. Weisst du schwarzt du (different version). Das leyderne Gebet. Eins ums andere. Der Sturm 15, No. 2, Berlin, 1924, pp. 87–92. *Poems.*

65 Arp, Hans. Die Traumkanzel. Der Sturm 15, No. 3, Berlin, 1924, pp. 168–189. *Poem.*

66 Arp, Hans. Liedertafel. De Stijl 6, No. 10/11, ed. by Van Doesburg, Weimar, 1924/25, p. 148.

67 Arp, Hans. Marmelsteinbälge. Schneetlehem. Oesophage, No. 1, May 1925, Brussels. *4 poems, dated 1918, 1921.*

68 Arp, Hans. La médaille se lève . . . La Révolution surréaliste, No. 5, Paris, October 15, 1925, p. 23. *Poetic prose (part of 71). Original woodcut by Arp, p. 25.*

69 Arp, Hans. Die fahneflüchtigen Engel stürzen verhetzt herein. Manomètre, No. 8, ed. Emile Malespine, Lyon, December 1925. *Poem.*

70 Arp, Hans. Das lichtscheue Paradies. L'Esprit Nouveau, No. 1, ed. by Dermée and M. Seuphor, Paris, 1925. *Poems. Reproduction of a relief by Arp.*

71 Arp, Hans. Schneetlehem. The Little Review, London, Spring/Summer 1926, p. 27. *Poems.*

72 Arp, Hans. Introduction. In: Max Ernst. Histoire Naturelle, Paris, 1926. *Poetic prose.*

73 Arp, Hans. Schnurrmilch. De Stijl 7, ed. by Van Doesburg, Paris, 1926, pp. 9/10. *Poems.*

74 Arp, Hans. Die gestiefelte(n) Steine. De Stijl, No. 79–84, ed. Van Doesburg, Paris, 1927, pp. 72–76. *Für Wilhelm Fraenger. Für Sophie Taeuber-Arp. Für C. Giedion-Welcker. Für Theo van Doesburg. Poems.*

75 Arp, Hans. Das lichtscheue Paradies, 1–8. De Stijl 7, No. 75/76, pp. 45/46; No. 77, pp. 79/80; No. 78, pp. 93/94. 1926/1927, Paris, No. 85/86, pp. 103–106, Paris, 1927/1928. *Poems.*

76 Arp, Hans. Cher Monsieur Brzekowski. L'Art Contemporain, No. 3, ed. Brzekowski, Paris, n. d. (ca. 1930), p. 102. *Cover by Arp. Reproductions of reliefs.*

77 Kunstsalon Wolfsberg, Production Paris. Zurich, 1930. *Catalogue of exhibition. Cover by Arp.*

78 Goll, Yvan. Die siebente Rose. Poésie & Co., Paris, n. d. (1930?). *Cover by Arp.*

79 Arp, Hans. Ich bin in Strassburg geboren . . . Der entthronte Tag. Cahiers Alsaciens et Lorrains 6, No. 8/9, 1931, p. 116. *Poems.*

80 Brzekowski, Jan. Kilométrage de la peinture contemporaine 1908–1930. Librairie Fischbacher, Paris, 1931. *Cover with two drawings (front and back) by Arp.*

81 Arp, Hans. Notes from a diary. Transition, No. 21. The Service Press, The Hague, March 1932. *Translated into English by E. Jolas. Cover (front and back) by Arp.*

82 Arp, Hans. Le style éléphant contre le style bidet. 2. 14. 33. Editions Cahiers d'Art, No. 1, Paris, March 1933, p. 14. *Essay.*

83 Arp, Hans. L'air est une racine. Le Surréalisme au service de la révolution 6. Paris, 1933, p. 33. *4 drawings by Arp.*

84 Violette Nozières. Editions Nicolas Flamel, Brussels, 1933 (Paris, José Corti, dépositaire). *Text by Breton, Char, and others. Illustrations by Arp, Dali, Tanguy and others.*

85 Brzekowski, Jan-Grenkamp-Kornfeld. Pri l'moderna arto. Literaturo mondo, Budapest, 1933. *Cover drawing by Arp.*

86 Brzekowski, Jan. Wdrugiej osobie poezje. Lodz (?), n. d. (1933). *Drawing on cover and 9 drawings by Arp.*

87 23 gravures de Arp, Calder, Chirico, Erni (etc.). Editions G. Orobitz et Cie., Paris, 1935. *Text by Anatole Jakovski. Original etching by Arp.*

88 Arp, Hans. Tibiis canere (Zurich 1915–1920). XXe Siècle, No. 1, March 1938, pp. 41–44. *Prose. First version, in French, of Dadaland. Cf. No. 113.*

89 Arp, Hans. Porte-nuage. L'âge l'éclair la main et la feuille. Transition, No. 27, pp. 12/13. The Service Press, The Hague, (April-May 1938.) *Poems.*

90 Arp, Hans. Manchas en el vacio. Total, San Diego, Chile, 1938. *Translation of: Des taches dans le vide.*

91 Brzekowski, Jan. Nuits végétales, avec un papier déchiré et interprété par Arp. Editions G. L. M., Paris, 1938. *220 copies, of which 20 are numbered constituting a special edition.*

92 XXe Siècle, No. 4. Paris, Christmas 1938. *Original graphic work by Arp.*

93 Arp, Hans. A fleur des fleurs. Les Saisons leurs astérisques et leurs pions. Plastique No. 4, Paris–New York, 1939, pp. 18–21. *6 poems.*

94 Arp, Hans. Bagarre de fruits. L'Usage de la Parole, No. 1, Paris, 12. 6. 1939, p. 6. *3 poems: Quelles sont ces manières de tête de mort (unpublished fragment). Eh' bien voilà. La langue ne vaut rien pour parler.*

95 Arp, Hans. Le squelette en vacances. Plastique, No. 5, 1939, pp. 2/3. *Chapter IV from: L'Homme qui a perdu son squelette. Novel by Arp, Carrington, Duchamp, Eluard, Hugnet, Prassinos, Ernst etc. Prose.*

96 Galerie Jeanne Bucher. (Invitation.) Paris, May 1939. *Cover: 7 drawings by Arp.*

97 Hugnet, Georges. Les chevaliers d'industrie. L'Usage de la Parole 1, No. 3, 1940, pp. 37/38. *Drawings by Arp.*

98 Arp, Hans. Le grand sadique à tout casser. In: La conquête du monde par l'image. Editions de la Main à Plume, Paris, 1942. *Prose.*

99 10 origin. Allianz-Verlag, Zurich, 1942. *Text by Arp: Depuis le temps des cavernes. Original woodcut by Arp. Edition of 100 portfolios, each with one signed woodcut or lithograph by 10 artists (Arp, Bill, Domela, etc.).*

100 Hugnet, Georges. La Sphère de sable. Aux dépens de Robert-J. Godet, Paris, 1943. (Collection: Pour mes amis, II.) *Drawings by Arp. Edition of 199 copies. Of these 3 are on China and 20 on Lafuma paper. Binding with original relief by Arp, drawings on vélin paper appended as loose leaves.*

101 Arp, Hans. Histoire arabesque. Vrille, No. 1, Paris, 7. 25. 1945, pp. 82/83. *Poem.*

102 Arp, Hans. Vite une tranche de terre... Les roses et les étoiles. Tu étais claire et calme. abstrakt + konkret, No. 6, special issue devoted to the Arp–Taeuber-Arp exhibition, in the Galerie des Eaux-Vives, Zurich, 1945. *Poems. Cover (woodcut) and 2 original woodcuts by Arp.*

103 Giedion-Welcker, Carola. Die neue Realität bei Guillaume Apollinaire. Benteli, Bern-Bümpliz, 1945. *Cover and title page by Arp.*

104 Arp, Hans. (Poems.) In: Carola Giedion-Welcker, Poètes à l'écart, Anthologie der Abseitigen. Benteli, Bern-Bümpliz, 1946, pp. 167–178. *Contents: Andante. Opus null. Schneetlehem. Westöstliche Rosen. Aus den Worten tauchen die Lippen empor. Die Augen sind Kränze aus Erde. Die Flammen füttern den Tod. Des taches dans le vide. Sophie. Joie noire. Les saisons de l'horloge de la fraise des animaux veloutés et du berceau.*

105 Tzara, Tristan. Vingt-cinq-et-un-poèmes. Collection L'Age d'Or, Editions de la revue Fontaine, Paris, 1946. *12 reproductions of drawings by Arp. 10 copies on Madagascar, 25 on Arches, 150 on Alfa, 600 on Surglacé.*

106 Arp, Jean. Aisément à travers le tunnel de la matière. In: Catalogue of the Magnelli Exhibition, ed. René Drouin, Galerie Drouin, Paris, 1947, pp. 1–9. *Poem in prose.*

107 Arp, Jean, Art concret. Réalités Nouvelles, No. 1, Paris, 1947, p. 10. *Poem in prose.*

108 Arp, Jean. Il chante il chante. Cot cot cot. Je suis un cheval. Les Quatre Vents, No. 8, Paris, 1947, pp. 22–25. *Poems.*

109 Arp, Jean. Le monde du souvenir et du rêve. In: Le Surréalisme en 1947, Editions Pierre à Feu (Galerie Maeght), Paris, 1947, pp. 69–70. *Essay on Sophie Taeuber-Arp, poem in prose. Special edition, numbered, with 2 original woodcuts by Arp.*

110 Arp, Jean. L'Oeuf de Kiesler et la salle des superstitions. Cahiers d'Art 22, Paris, 1947, pp. 281–286. *Poem in prose.*

111 Arp, Jean. Tension de sol. In: Galerie Allendy, George L. K. Morris Exhibition, Paris, November 1947. *Poem in prose.*

112 Arp, Jean and Camille Bryen. L'araignée brode sa toile... In: Galerie Allendy, Exhibition "Tapisseries et Broderies Abstraites", Paris, 1948. *Preface (poetic prose).*

113 Arp, Hans. Dadaland. Atlantis, Special issue, Zurich, 1948, pp. 275/276. *Cf. 88. Enlarged German version.*

114 Arp, Hans. Introduction to Max Ernst's Natural History. In: Max Ernst, Beyond Painting. The Documents of Modern Art. Wittenborn, Schultz, Inc. New York, 1948. *Poem in prose. Translated into English by Ralph Manheim.*

115 Arp, Hans. (Kurt Schwitters). Galerie d'Art Moderne, Basel, 1948. *Poetic prose (Invitation to Kurt Schwitters' memorial exhibition).*

116 Arp, Hans. Sophie Taeuber-Arp. In: Georg Schmidt, Sophie Taeuber-Arp. Holbein Verlag, Basel, 1948. *German version, pp. 23–27, French version pp. 28–32.*

117 Arp, Hans. Die Welt der Erinnerung und des Traumes. Violettes Rouges. Palaestra, No. 8, Holland, 1948. *German version of poem in No. 109.*

118 Arp, Jean. Kurt Schwitters. L'insonore bleu. In: De l'humour à la terreur – Hommage à Schwitters. K – revue de la poésie, No. 3, Paris, May 1949, pp. 34/35, 45. *Poetic prose. Poem.*

119 Arp, Hans. Firi. Maurulam Katapult i lemm i lamm. In: Poésie de Mots Inconnus, ed. by Iliazd for Le Degré 41, Paris, 1949. *Poems and original graphic works by prominent artists. The two Lautgedichte by Arp 1924 (unpublished), and 1927. Frontispiece woodcut by Arp and Camille Bryen. Collector's de luxe edition, single sheets on various expensive papers, wrapped in parchment.*

120 Arp, Jean. Kandinsky, Sophie Taeuber-Arp. ... et des étoiles. Place Blanche. In: L'Art Abstrait, ses origines, ses premiers maîtres, ed. Michel Seuphor. Maeght, Paris, 1949, pp. 99/100, 109/110. *Reproductions, portrait. 2 original woodcuts and cover by Arp. First edition of 995 numbered copies. Second edition, Paris, 1950.*

121 Arp, Hans. Oasis de pureté. In: Vordemberge-Gildewart, Epoque néerlandaise,- Editions Duwaer, Amsterdam, 1949. *Preface. Translated into French by Robert Valançay after: Reine Eilande, from: Onze peintres vus par Arp. Cf. No. 20.*

122 Arp, Hans. quatre piraine. Paris, 1949. *Lautgedicht für Bozzolini und Righetti. Album with 10 linoleum cuts.*

123 Arp, Hans. Francis Picabia. Art d'aujourd'hui, No. 6, Paris, January 1950. *Poetic prose.*

124 Arp, Jean. Formes. Art d'aujourd'hui, No. 11/12, Paris, May-June 1950. *Poem.*

125 Arp, Jean. (Poems). Derrière le Miroir, No. 33, November 1950. *Contains: Sophie rêvait, Sophie peignait, Sophie dansait. Tu étais claire et calme. Yeux de cire. Et frappe et frappe et frappe. Elle devient une tête. L'eau reste vide. 3 original lithographs by Arp.*

126 J. Arp – S. Delaunay – A. Magnelli – S. Taeuber-Arp. Les Nourritures Terrestres. Paris, 1950. *Album with 10 color lithographs. Numbered 1–150 and I–XV, all copies signed.*

127 Arp, Jean. Et frappe et frappe et frappe. L'eau reste vide. Elle devient une tête. In: Humour poétique, 50 inédits. La Nef, No. 71/72. Editions du Sagittaire, Paris, December 1950 – January 1951. *Poems. Biographical data pp. 17–19, written by Arp. Definition of Humor by Arp. Poem for Arp by Max Jacob (1915).*

128 Arp, Jean. Roses pour Rose. Editions PAB, Alès, January–February 1951.

129 Arp, Jean. Message de la sculpture. XXe Siècle, Nouvelle Série, No. 1, Paris, June 1951. *Original lithograph by Arp.*

130 Arp, Hans. Dans le vide (à Theo van Doesburg). Leere Fülle. Essence, Monatsschrift für Originalgraphik und Dichtung, Zurich, July-August 1951, p. 2. *Unpublished poems composed in 1930 and 1950.*

131 Arp, Jean. Isabelle et les assiettes. Catalogue of exhibition L'Assiette Peinte. Christofle, Paris, November-December 1951. *Prose.*

132 Arp, Hans. Dada was not a farce. In: The Dada Painters and Poets. An Anthology, ed. by Robert Motherwell. Wittenborn, Schultz, Inc., New York, 1951, pp. 293-294. *Written in 1949, translated into English by Ralph Manheim. Also contains: Notes from a Dada diary, and Sophie (1946), translated into English by Ralph Manheim.*

133 Arp, Jean. Les Hulbeck. Galerie des Deux Iles, Paris, 1951. *Text for invitation, poetic prose.*

134 Bryen, Camille. Temps Troué. Collection Le Soleil Noir, Paris, 1951. Poems. – Drawings, original woodcuts, torn papers by Arp. *320 copies, of which 20 on Annam de Rives with a proof of a portrait déchiré and a set of the woodcuts on separate loose sheets, and a dessin périgraphique (dabbed drawing finished by hand).*

135 Arp, Jean. Hans Richter. XXe Siècle, Nouvelle Série, No. 2, Paris, January 1952. *Poetic prose.*

136 Arp, Jean. Le langage intérieur. XXe Siècle, Nouvelle Série, No. 3, Paris, June 1952. *Poetic prose. Cf. No. 263.*

137 Arp, Hans. Ainsi se ferma la cercle. In: Témoignage pour l'Art Abstrait. Edition Art d'aujourd'hui, Paris, 1952. *Poetic prose. Biographical notes. Photo portrait, reproductions. 1,500 numbered copies.*

138 Huelsenbeck, Richard. Die New Yorker Kantaten. Cantates New Yorkaises. European Art Documentation, Berggruen & Cie., Paris – New York, 1952. *6 drawings and cover by Arp.*

139 Picabia. Fleurmontée. PAB (privately printed), Alés, 1952. *Poem. Planimetric sculpture by Arp.*

140 Arp, Hans. Die Ebene. Sophie. Das Jagdschlößchen. Weltstimmen, No. 3, Stuttgart, March 1953, pp. 135/136. *Poetic prose.*

141 Arp, Hans. (Selection of German poems). Neue Literarische Welt 4, No. 6, 3. 25. 1953, p. 8. *Unpublished poems from: Behaarte Herzen (1920), Die ungewisse Welt (1939-1945), Der vierblättrige Stern, Blatt um Feder um Blatt.*

142 Arp, Jean. (Poems.) In: Anthologie der französischen Dichtung von Nerval bis zur Gegenwart – Anthologie de la Poésie française de Nerval à nos jours. V. II: Die Zeitgenossen – Les Contemporains. Ed. by Flora Klee-Palyi. Limes-Verlag, Wiesbaden, 1953, pp. 92-99. *Contains: L'étoile ternit. Vite une tranche de terre. Une goutte d'homme. La langue ne vaut rien pour parler. Les fleurs sont noires de joie. With*

German version by Fritz Usinger. Veines noires. Translated into German by Hans Arp and Marguerite Hagenbach.

143 Arp, Jean. Jumeaux de sève. Contre ces nuages. Vite, vite. En chair et en os. Ils ont assez balancé. Cahiers d'Art 18, No. 1, Paris, 1953.
Unpublished poems. Reproductions.

144 Arp, Hans. Immer wandelt sich die Schönheit. In: Trunken von Gedichten – Eine Anthologie geliebter deutscher Verse. Ed. by Georg Gerster. Verlag der Arche, Zurich, 1953. *First printing, poetic prose. Cf. No. 264.*

145 Arp, Hans. Unter den Wolkentischen. In: Surrealistische Publikationen, ed. by Edgar Jené and Max Hölzer, n. d. (1953? 1954?). *First publication.*

146 Art d'aujourd'hui, Série 4, No. 6, August 1953. *Cover by Arp.*

147 Arp, Jean. Danger de Mort. XXe Siècle, No. 4, Paris, January 1954. *Essay. Drawings, 2 original woodcuts by Arp.*

148 Arp, Jean. Michel Seuphor. Catalogue. Dessins à Lacunes by Michel Seuphor. Berggruen & Cie., Paris, January 1954. *Preface (poetic prose).*

149 Arp, Hans. Michel Seuphor zeichnet schon seit langer Zeit. Galerie d'Art moderne, Basel, 1954.
German version of No. 148.

150 Arp, Hans. Die Schönheit versank nicht. Sophie tanzte. Spirale 1, Bern, n. d., (1954?). *Linoleum cut.*

151 Arp, Hans. Point blanc. Vert comme la mousse d'éclair. Spirale 3, Bern, n. d., (1954?). *From: Le Siège de l'air.*

152 Breton, André. Adieu ne plaise. PAB (privately printed), Alès, January 1954. *Photo déchirée by Arp.*

153 Huelsenbeck, Richard. Die Antwort der Tiefe. Limes-Verlag, Wiesbaden, 1954. *Poems. – 7 reproductions of collages by Arp.*

154 Zervos, Christian. La situation faite au dessin dans l'Art Contemporain. Cahiers d'Art 29, special issue, Paris, 1954. *Drawing by Arp.*

155 Arp, Jean. Antoine Poncet. Carreau, Lausanne, March 1955. *Poetic prose.*

156 Arp, Jean. Francis Picabia est un Christophe Colomb de l'art, in memoriam Francis Picabia. Edition Orbes, Paris, 4. 20. 1955. *English translation: Francis Picabia is the Christopher Columbus, in the catalogue of the Picabia exhibition, Rose Fried Gallery, New York.*

157 Arp, Jean. La colonne sans fin. Hommage à Brancusi. Cahiers d'Art 30, Paris, 1955. *Poem.*

158 Arp, Hans. Opus Null. Sein Kinderhut tanzt. In: Lyrik des expressionistischen Jahrzehnts, intr. by Gottfried Benn. Limes-Verlag, Wiesbaden, 1955. *The second poem incomplete.*

159 Arp, Hans. Werkstattfabeln und Traumgedanken. Aus "Hundert und ein Gedicht". Das Bilderhaus, No. 5, Kunstverein Freiburg i. B., 1955, pp. 5–9, 10–12. *First publications. Cover, original woodcut by Arp.*

160 Arp, Hans. Gedichte aus: Träume und Projekte. Texte und Zeichen 1, No. 4, Berlin 1955, pp. 431-435. *2 reproductions of woodcuts by Arp.*

161 Arp, Hans. Die bunten Bälle. Der Jäger im tannengrünen Rock. Lecke Sterne. Profile, No. 5/6, ed. by Rudolf Wittkopf and Dieter Wyss, n. d. (1955). *Unpublished poems. Original woodcut.*

162 Arp, Jean and Camille Bryen. Colloque de Meudon sur les collages. XXe Siècle, No. 6, Paris, January 1956. *Collage, pochoir: Configuration 1955.*

163 Art News, New York, February 1956. *Cover is color reproduction of: Symétrique aux Flocons du Hasard, Collage 1955 by Arp.*

164 Benoît, P. A. Jour. PAB (privately printed), Pour la St. Jean. Alès, 1955. *Original woodcut by Arp.*

165 Frey, Alexander M. Kleine Menagerie. Limes-Verlag, Wiesbaden, 1955. *Introduction by Thomas Mann. 10 reproductions of woodcuts by Arp. 70 copies on handmade paper, signed by Frey and Arp, and printed from the original blocks.*

166 10 Jahre Galerie d'Art moderne Bâle. Privately printed, Basel, 1. 22. 1955. *Portfolio with 10 original lithographs, of which one is by Arp. 125 numbered copies, signed by artists. 25 numbered and signed proofs of lithograph sold separately.*

167 XXe Siècle, No. 5, June 1955. *Cover by Arp.*

168 Tzara, Tristan. Parler Seul. Collection Caractères, Paris, 1955. *15 copies contain a woodcut by Arp.*

169 Arp, Hans and Kurt Schwitters. Le dé. Phantomas 3, No. 6, Brussels, spring 1956, pp. 10/11. *Translation from the German by Paule Mévisse.*

170 Arp, Hans. Franz Müllers Drahtfrühling. Quadrum, No. 1, Brussels, May 1956. *Recollections of Kurt Schwitters.*

171 Arp, Hans. Beiträge zum 70. Geburtstag.

In: Ivo Hauptmann, ed. by Rolf Italiaander. Freie Akademie der Künste, Hamburg, 1956, pp. 21/22. *Recollections of the Weimar period. Originally was to be entitled: Mit einem Cypriotenstock.*

172 Arp, Jean. Celui qui veut abattre un nuage. In: Témoignage pour la sculpture abstraite (Arp, Bloc, Descombin etc.). Editions A. A. et Denise René, Paris, 1956. *From: Werkstattfabeln, translated into French by Michel Seuphor. Cf. No. 245.*

173 Arp, Hans. Häuser. Akzente, No. 5. Carl Hanser, Munich, 1956. *6 unpublished poems.*

174 Arp, Hans. Schwarze Eier. In: Flügel der Zeit, Deutsche Gedichte 1900–1950, ed. by Curt Hohoff, Fischer Bücherei, Frankfurt, 1956. *Reprinted from: Wortträume und schwarze Sterne.*

175 Eluard, Paul. Un poème dans chaque livre. Collection Ecrits et Gravures, ed.

Louis Broder, Paris, 1956. *Woodcut by Arp, VIII. For: Défense de savoir, 1927. 120 signed copies.*

176 Goll, Yvan. Multiple Femme. Collection Caractères, Bruno Durocher, Paris, 1956. *Poems. – Cover and 8 woodcuts by Arp. De luxe edition of 50 numbered copies.*

177 Puel, Gaston. Ce chant entre deux astres. Les Ecrivains Réunis, Armand Henneuse, Lyon, 1956. *2 reproductions of collages by Arp. 30 numbered copies on Vélin de Renage.*

178 Arp, Hans. Auf einem Bein. Auf einbeinigen Blumentischen. In: Das Gedicht, Jahrbuch zeitgenössischer Lyrik 1956–1957, ed. by Rudolf Ibel, Christian Wegner Verlag, Hamburg.

179 Arp, Jean. Encyclopédie Arpadienne. In: Art et Humour au XXe Siècle, XXe Siècle, No. 8, Paris, 1956/1957, pp. 13–16. *Little poems, 7 reproductions, 2 stencils.*

180 Arp, Hans. La Promenade, für Madja Ruperti und ihre Bilder. Van Diemen-Lilienfeld Galleries, New York, 3. 20.–4. 12. 1957. *Poetic prose.*

181 Arp, Hans. In memoriam Henri Solveen. Les dernières nouvelles d'Alsace, No. 110, Strassburg, 5. 12/13. 1957. *Poetic prose.*

182 Arp, Hans. Auf verschleierten Schaukeln. Akzente, No. 1, Carl Hanser Verlag, Munich, 1957, pp. 52–55. *Unpublished poems.*

183 Arp, Jean. Reflections of a Sculptor, Jean Arp replies to seven questions put to him by George L. K. Morris. In: The World of Abstract Art, The American Abstract Artists, George Wittenborn, Inc., New York, n. d. (1957), pp. 149–154. *Cover (papier déchiré) by Arp.*

184 Huelsenbeck, Richard. Mit Witz, Licht und Grütze, Auf den Spuren des Dadaismus. Limes Verlag, Wiesbaden, 1957. *Book cover (front and back), title page by Arp.*

C. Writings on Jean Arp

185 Alvard, J. Reliefs de Jean Arp. Cimaise, 2nd series, No. 7, June 1955.

186 A. P. I. A. W. Arp et Sophie Taeuber. Liège, 9. 19–10. 1. 1953. *Catalogue of exhibition. Preface by Michel Seuphor. First printing of the poem "Sophie" by Arp. Reproductions. Short biography.*

187 Ball, Hugo. Die Flucht aus der Zeit. Duncker & Humblot Verlag, Munich, 1927. Pp. 77, 79, 85, 90, 95, 98, 122, 151, 153, 157, 167, 169. *New edition: Verlag Josef Stocker, Lucerne, 1946.*

188 Baron, Jacques. Arp. Cahiers de Belgique 1, No. 6, July 1928, pp. 221–224. *6 reproductions.*

189 Bazin, Germain. Arp. L'Amour de l'Art 15, No. 3, March 1934. *Biographical and bibliographical notes. Also published in: Histoire de l'Art Contemporain, La peinture, ed. by René Huyghe. Alcan, Paris, 1935.*

190 Bell, Eleanor. Arp's Marbles and Bronzes. The Cincinnati Post, Cincinnati, 3. 5. 1949.

191 Bettini, Sergio. Jean Arp. La Biennale di Venezia, No. 19–20, 1954, p. 27.

192 La Biennale di Venezia. Lombroso Editore, Venice, 1954. *Text by Michel Seuphor: Jean Arp, pp. 227–230. Reprod. Nos. 66, 67.*

193 Bill, Max. Von der abstrakten zur konkreten Kunst: eine Einführung in Probleme der zeitgenössischen Kunst. Amphioxus 2, No. 3, 1946, pp. 5–8.

194 Bill, Max. Hans Arp. Die Weltwoche 15, No. 724, 9. 26. 1947. p. 5.

195 Bille, Ejler. Hans Arp. Nyt Tidskrift for Kunstindustri 1, No. 9, September 1937, pp. 159–161. *6 reproductions.*

196 Bille, Ejler. Hans Arp: utdaleser af Hans Arp. In: Picasso, Surrealisme, Abstrakt Kunst. Forlaget Helios, Copenhagen, 1945, pp. 169–1757. *7 reproductions, portrait.*

197 Bordier, Roger. L'Art et la Manière, une enquête sur la technique: Arp, les reliefs et le plâtre. Art d'aujourd'hui, 5th series, No. 4/5, Paris, May/June 1954. *Photographs of Arp's studio at Meudon.*

198 Breton, André. Le surréalisme et la peinture. Gallimard, Paris, 1928, pp. 69–72.

199 Breton, André. Hans Arp. Anthologie de l'humour noir. Editions du Sagittaire, Paris, 1940, pp. 226–228. *Contains Arp's poem "Bestiaire sans Prénom."*

200 Brion, Marcel. Art Abstrait. Albin Michel, Paris, 1956, pp. 168–171.

201 Bruguière, P. G. Arp. Cahiers d'Art 22, Paris, 1947, pp. 267–271.

202 Bruguière, P. G. Sur Arp. Derrière le Miroir, No. 33, November 1950. *Cf. No. 125.*

203 Bryen, Camille. Arp et le langage. Fontaine 8, No. 60, May 1947.

204 Bryen, Camille. Arpoétique. Documents 2, No. 18, Lausanne, March 1952, pp. 8–10.

205 Brzekowski, Jan. Hans Arp. Collection a. r., Lodz, 1936. *10 reproductions.*

206 Buffet-Picabia, Gabrielle. Jean Arp. abstrakt + konkret, No. 6, Galerie des Eaux-Vives, Zurich, 1945. *Special issue devoted to the Arp–Taeuber-Arp exhibition, Galerie des Eaux-Vives, 1945. Cf. No. 102.*

207 Buffet-Picabia, Gabrielle. Jean Arp. 34 pp., Collection L'Art abstrait. Les Presses Littéraires de France, Paris, 1952. *8 reproductions, portrait.*

208 Cathelin, Jean. De la Sincérité. Derrière le Miroir, No. 33, Paris, Nov. 1950. *Cf. 125.*

209 Clancier, Georges Emmanuel. De Rimbaud au Surréalisme. Edition Pierre Seghers, Paris, 1953, pp. 465–468.

210 Croxleÿ, Hubert. Hans Arp. Cahiers d'Art 3, No. 5/6, Paris, 1928, pp. 229/230. *9 reproductions.*

211 Croxleÿ, Hubert. Quelques considérations sur le problème plastique tel qu'il se pose pour Hans Arp. Centaure 3, 1928, pp. 36–38.

212 Current Biography: Hans Arp. Who's News and Why 15, No. 5. H. W. Wilson Co., New York, May 1954, pp. 7–9.

213 Debrunner, Hugo and others. Wir entdecken Kandinsky. Series: In Medias Res, Origo-Verlag, Zurich (1947?). *Pp. 55–57: Conversation between Hans Arp and Debrunner. Interpretation of a conversation with Arp about Kandinsky.*

214 Degand, Léon. Arp, un terroriste constructif. Juin, Paris, 11. 19. 1946.

215 Degand, Léon. J. Arp. Art d'aujourd'hui 3, No. 1, Paris, December 1951. *Biography, essay, photo portrait, reproductions.*

216 Degand, Léon. Arp. Aujourd'hui, No. 3, Paris, June 1955.

217 Degand, Léon. Arp-Collages, Aujourd'hui, No. 6, Paris, January 1956.

218 Descargues, Pierre. Jean Arp, retour des U. S. A. Arts, No. 271, Paris, 7. 14. 1950.

219 Descargues, Pierre. Jean Arp. Arts, No. 285, Paris, 11. 17. 1950.

220 Descargues, Pierre. Jean Arp et la forme pure. Arts, Paris, 10. 5. 1951.

221 Dictionnaire biographique français contemporain. Arp (Jean). Editions Pharos, Paris, 1950, p. 28. *Portrait.*

222 Dictionnaire de la peinture moderne. Arp (by Michel Seuphor). Editions Fernand Hazan, Paris, 1954, pp. 8–10. *2 reproductions.*

223 Doesburg, Theo van. Notices sur l'Aubette à Strasbourg. De Stijl, No. 87–89, Paris, 1928, pp. 7/8, 11–14.

224 Einstein, Carl. Die Kunst des 20. Jahrhunderts. Propyläen-Kunstgeschichte 16. Propyläen-Verlag, Berlin, 1928, 2nd edition, pp. 128/129, 624–627, 649.

225 Einstein, Carl. L'enfance néolithique. Documents 2, No. 8, Paris, 1930, pp. 35–43. *9 reproductions.*

226 Eluard, Paul. Arp (poem for). In: Capitale de la douleur, Editions de la Nouvelle Revue Française, Librairie Gallimard, Paris, 1926, p. 132. *Translated in: Contemporary Poetry and Prose, No. 2, 6. 20. 1936.*

227 Erdmann-Czapski, Veronika. Hans Arp "Pyramidenrock"; zur Entwicklungspsychologie des Dadaismus. Das Kunstblatt 10, June 1926, pp. 218–221.

228 Ernst, Max. Arp. Littérature 3, No. 19, Paris, 5. 12. 1921, pp. 10–12.

229 Estienne, Charles. Arp, poète. Art d'aujourd'hui, No. 10/11, Paris, 1950.

230 Fernandez, Justino. Prometeo, ensayo sobre pintura contemporanea. Editorial Porrua, Mexico, D. F., 1945, pp. 32/33.

231 Flake, Otto. Ja und Nein. Roman. S. Fischer-Verlag, Berlin, 1920, pp. 76–79, 81, 111–116, 123/124, 145–147, 163/164, 176–178, 238–241.

232 Frey, A. M. Die Kunst Hans Arps. Nationalzeitung, Basel, 6. 25. 1949.

233 Frey, A. M. Bücher von übermorgen: Hans Arp. Weltstimmen, No. 2, Stuttgart, February 1953, p. 93. *Photo portrait.*

234 Frey, A. M. Versblumen auf den Traumwiesen Arpscher Lyrik . . . Neue Literarische Welt 4, No. 6, 3. 25. 1953. *Cf. No. 141.*

235 Frey, A. M. Die Lyrik des Plastikers Hans Arp. Literaturkalender 1955, ed. Hartfrid Voss, Langewiesche Brandt-Verlag, Ebenhausen near Munich. V. 4, 1954, pp. 110/111. *Biographical note, photo portrait.*

236 Arp und die elementare Gestaltung. G (periodical), No. 4, Berlin, March 1926, p. 9.

237 Galerie ars felix. arp + bissier. Arbon, 8.4–9.2.1956. *Catalogue of exhibition. Lithographs, pen drawings, woodcuts, collages. Biographical data. Photo portrait.*

238 Galerie d'Art Moderne. Arp-Bryen. Basel, 11. 16. 1946. *Text of the invitation to the opening of the exhibition by Camille Bryen: Les lois du hasard.*

239 Galerie Bing. Jean Arp – Sonia Delaunay – A. Magnelli – S. Taeuber-Arp. Paris, 1954. *Catalogue of exhibition. Preface by Gabrielle Buffet-Picabia.*

240 Galerie des Deux Iles. Un Quatuor (Sonia Delaunay – Sophie Taeuber – Alberto Magnelli – Jean Arp). Paris, 1948. *Catalogue of exhibition. Preface by Michel Seuphor: Un Quatuor.*

241 Galerie Goemans. (Exhibition of collages by Arp, and others). Paris, 1930. *Catalogue of exhibition. Text by Louis Aragon: La peinture au défi.*

242 Galerie Herbert Herrmann. josef albers – hans arp – max bill. Stuttgart, July-August 1948. *Catalogue of exhibition. Text by Hans Hildebrandt.*

243 Galerie Edouard Loeb. Paris, 5. 14. 1955. *Text of the invitation to the opening of the exhibition by Camille Bryen: Arp tourne autour de la terre . . .*

244 Galerie Montaigne. Salon Dada. International Exhibition, Paris, June, 1922. *5 reproductions. Poem by Arp: Devant la chambre des fileuses. Translated from: die wolkenpumpe. De luxe edition, numbered copies.*

245 Galerie Denise René. 1. Salon de la Sculpture Abstraite. Catalogue: Témoignage pour la sculpture abstraite (Arp, Bloc, Descombin, etc.). Editions A. A. et Denise René, Paris, 1956. *Preface by Pierre Guéguen. Photo portrait. 7 reproductions. Text by Arp: Celui qui veut abattre un nuage. Cf. No. 172.*

246 Galerie Surréaliste. Arp. Paris, 10.24–11. 10., 11.21–12.9. 1927. *Preface by André Breton. 4 reproductions.*

247 Gallery Art of this Century. Arp. New York, February 1944. *Essay on Arp by Max Ernst.*

248 Gallery Buchholz. Jean Arp. New York, 1.18–2.12. 1949. *Text by Jean Cathelin: On Sincerity, The Work of Jean Arp. Text by Arp: Our works are structures of lines, from: On My Way. Cover by Arp.*

249 Gallery Sidney Janis. Jean Arp + Sophie Taeuber. New York, 1.30–2.25. 1950. *Preface by Michel Seuphor: Sophie Taeuber-Arp and Jean Arp, translated into English by Martin James.*

250 Gallery Curt Valentin. Jean Arp. *Preface by Arp, translated into English by William Crumley. Biographical notes. Drawing on cover by Arp.*

251 Gasch, Sebastià. Hans Arp a Barcelona. Mirardor, Barcelona, 9. 1. 1932.

252 Gertz, Ulrich. Plastik der Gegenwart. Rembrandt-Verlag, Berlin, 1953. Pp. 22, 30, 32, 36, 38. *3 reproductions.*

253 Gheerbrandt, Alain. Jean Arp ou la réalité. La Gazette des lettres 3, No. 39, Paris, June 1947. *On: Le Siège de l'air.*

254 Giedion-Welcker, Carola. Die Funktion der Sprache in der heutigen Dichtung. Transition, No. 22, The Hague, 1933. Pp. 93–95.

255 Giedion-Welcker, Carola. Modern plastic art: elements of reality, volume and disintegration. H. Girsberger, Zurich, 1937, pp. 11, 12, 86, 92, 96. *6 reproductions. Quotations from the Tagebuch (1931), biographical appendix p. 152. Also published under the title: Moderne Plastik, Elemente der Wirklichkeit, Masse und Auflockerung, 1937.*

256 Giedion-Welcker, Carola. Über das Gedichtbändchen: Hans Arp, 1924, 1925, 1926, 1943. Werk 31, fasc. 8, Winterthur, August 1944, p. XXVI.

257 Giedion-Welcker, Carola. Contemporary Sculptors, IV, Jean Arp. Horizon 14, No. 82, London, October 1946, pp. 232–239. *15 reproductions, essay on Arp's artistic development including his Dada period.*

258 Giedion-Welcker, Carola. Poètes à l'écart – Anthologie der Abseitigen. Benteli, Bern-Bümpliz, 1946, pp. 165–178. *Cf. No. 104.*

259 Giedion-Welcker, Carola. Über die Ausstellung Jean Arp – Camille Bryen in der Galerie d'Art Moderne in Basel, 11.16–12. 5. 1946. Werk 34, fasc. 11, Winterthur, January 1947, pp. 4, 5.

260 Giedion-Welcker, Carola. Über die Holzschnittmappe: Hans Arp "Elemente". Werk 37, fasc. 12, Winterthur, December 1950, p. 182.

261 Giedion-Welcker, Carola. Hans Arp. Das Kunstblatt 14, December 1950, pp. 372–375. *Reproductions.*

262 Giedion-Welcker, Carola. Urelement und Gegenwart in der Kunst Hans Arps. Werk 39, fasc. 5, May 1952, pp. 164–172. *Reproductions.*

263 Giedion-Welcker, Carola. Le retour aux éléments dans la poésie et la peinture. XXe Siècle, No. 3 (double), Paris, June 1952. *Pp. 44/45 on Arp. Cf. No. 136.*

264 Giedion-Welcker, Carola. (Commentary on a poem by Arp.) In: Trunken von Gedichten. Eine Anthologie geliebter deutscher Verse, ed. by Georg Gerster, Verlag der Arche, Zurich, 1953, pp. 135–141. *Cf. No. 144.*

265 Giedion-Welcker, Carola. Plastik des 20. Jahrhunderts. Verlag Gerd Hatje, Stuttgart, 1955. Pp. XIII/XIV, XVI, XXIII, XXV/XXVI, XXX, 100–109, 136, 137, 158, 258, 259. *Reproductions. Also published under the title: Contemporary Sculpture, An Evolution in Volume and Space. Documents of Modern Art 12, George Wittenborn, Inc., New York, 1955.*

266 Giedion-Welcker, Carola. Schwitters und Arp in Bern, Résumé der Ansprache bei der Vernissage in der Kunsthalle Bern. Weltwoche, 4. 20. 1956.

267 Gindertael, R. V. Liberté de Jean Arp. Combat 10, No. 2266, Paris, 10. 16. 1951.

268 Göpel, Erhard. Chiffren der Moderne. Merkur 8, fasc. 12, No. 82, December 1954, pp. 1199–1200.

269 Guggenheim, Peggy (ed.). Art of this century: objects, drawings, photographs, paintings, sculpture, collages, 1910 to 1942. Art of this century, New York, 1942. *Catalogue of the permanent exhibition, lists 3 works by Arp. Biographical data p. 101. Essay by Arp: abstract art, concrete art, pp. 29–31. English text of the poem: L'Usage de la parole, p. 101.*

270 Haftmann, Werner. Malerei im 20. Jahrhundert. Prestel-Verlag, Munich, 1954–1955. V. 1, pp. 246–263, 482, Plate 21; v. 2, pp. 196, 209.

271 Hauptmann, Ivo. Begegnung mit Hans Arp. Die Zeit, Hamburg, February 1955.

272 Hildebrandt, Hans. Die Kunst des 19. und 20. Jahrhunderts. Athenaion, Akademische Verlagsgesellschaft, Potsdam, n. d. Pp. 281, 284, 424, 425.

273 Höllerer, Walter. Transit, Lyrikbuch der Jahrhundertmitte. Suhrkamp-Verlag, Frankfurt, 1956. *Biographical and bibliographical data. Poems from: Wortträume und schwarze Sterne. Auf einem Bein.*

274 Hôtel de Ville. Sept Pionniers de la Sculpture moderne. Yverdon, 7. 18–9. 28. 1954. *Catalogue of exhibition. Text by Michel Seuphor: Jean Arp. Notes on the works exhibited by Marguerite Hagenbach. 2 reproductions.*

275 Huelsenbeck, Richard. Die Arbeiten von Hans Arp. In: Dada 3, Zurich, 12.7.1918. *English translation by author in the Library of the Museum of Modern Art, New York. Cf. No. 44.*

276 Huelsenbeck, Richard. Dada siegt: eine Bilanz des Dadaismus. Malik-Verlag, Berlin, 1920, pp. 5, 6, 13–16, 18–20, 22, 24, 25.

277 Huelsenbeck, Richard. Der Plastiker Hans Arp. Neue Zeitung, No. 212, Berlin, 9. 12. 1954.

278 Huelsenbeck, Richard. Mit Licht, Witz und Grütze, Auf den Spuren des Dadaismus. Limes-Verlag, Wiesbaden, 1957, pp. 17, 27–32, 37, 44, 53, 56–61, 63–66, 74–76, 79, 80, 86, 108, 110, 125, 135, 144. *Cf. No. 184.*

279 Hugnet, Georges. Fantastic art, dada, surrealism. The Museum of Modern Art, distributed by Simon and Schuster, New York, 1947, 3d ed., pp. 16–18, 226, and passim. *Essays. 10 reproductions.*

280 Hugnet, Georges. L'Esprit dada dans la peinture. Cahiers d'Art 7, Paris, 1932, pp. 57, 60, 62, 64, 282, 284, 285, 358–364, and Cahiers d'Art 9, Paris, 1934, pp. 109–114.

281 Hugnet, Georges. Jean Arp. Preuves 4, No. 44, Paris, October 1954, pp. 44–53. *Unpublished French poems by Arp.*

282 Hugnet, Georges. L'aventure Dada (1916–1922). Galerie de l'Institut, Paris, 1957. *With an introduction by Tristan Tzara. Chapter "Zurich" pp. 18–32. Reproductions.*

283 Jakovski, Anatole. Arp, Calder, Hélion, Miro, Pevsner, Seligmann. Jacques Povolozsky, Paris, n. d., pp. 3–10.

284 Jean, Marcel. Jalons d'Arp. Les Lettres nouvelles 4, No. 35, Paris, February 1956, pp. 180–195. *Reproductions of original graphic works by Arp.*

285 Jené, Edgar. Hans Arp. Der Plan 2, No. 4, Vienna, 1947, p. 291, 292.

286 Kern, Walter. Zu Hans Arps "Vogelmaske", Gedanken und Aufsätze über Kunst. Oprecht-Verlag, Zurich–New York, 1940. *First version in: Das Kunstblatt, 1930.*

287 Kestner-Gesellschaft. Hans Arp – Sophie Taeuber-Arp. Hannover, 1.7–2.13.1955. *Catalogue of exhibition. Preface by Alfred Hentzen. Frontispiece: Lithograph by Arp (1932).*

288 Kuenzi, André. Arp et Schwitters à Berne. La Gazette littéraire, Gazette de Lausanne, April 1956, pp. 28, 29. *Reproductions.*

289 Kunsthalle Bern. Hans Arp – Kurt Schwitters. Bern, 4.7–5. 6. 1956. *Catalogue of exhibition. Preface by Franz Meyer. Biographical notes by Hans Bolliger.*

290 Kunsthaus Zurich. Begründer der modernen Plastik. Zurich, 11.27 –end December 1954. *Catalogue of exhibition. Text by Arp: Der Keim einer neuen Plastik, from: On my way. Bibliography, biography by Hans Bolliger. Notes on the works exhibited by Marguerite Hagenbach. Reproductions.*

291 Kunstnerforbundet. International nutidskunst: konstruktivisme, neo-plasticisme, abstrakt kunst, surrealisme. Oslo, 9. 16–10. 2. 1938(?). *Catalogue of exhibition. Short biography and bibliography. Reproduction. Exhibition arranged by Bjerke-Petersen, Arp, and Taeuber-Arp.*

292 Kunstsalon Wolfsberg. Arp, Berger, Egger, Helbig, Segal. Zurich, 1917. *Catalogue of exhibition. Preface (by W. Jollos).*

293 Kunstsalon Wolfsberg. Die neue Kunst. Zurich, 1918. *Catalogue of exhibition. Preface by W. Jollos. Cf. No. 45.*

294 Leiris, Michel. Exposition Hans Arp Galerie Goemans. Documents 1, No. 6, Paris, pp. 340–342. *2 reproductions.*

295 Lewis, Jean. Architectural Design 27, February 1957, pp. 62, 63. *Reproductions.*

296 Librairie La Hune. Arcadie d'Arp. Paris, October 1951. *Catalogue of exhibition. Text by Michel Seuphor. Bibliography. 100 copies constitute a special edition, with an original woodcut by Arp.*

297 Limes-Lesebuch. Zehn Jahre Verlagsarbeit. Limes-Verlag. Wiesbaden, 1955. *Poem: Reif zum Aussteigen, from: Auf einem Bein. 2 reproductions.*

298 Lopez, Torres. Hans Arp. Gaceta de Arte 3, No. 24, March 1934, p. 1. *3 reproductions.*

299 Marchiori, Guiseppe. Scultura Moderna. La Biennale di Venezia, No. 23, Venice, January 1955, pp. 9, 10. *Text by Arp: Jalons. Drawing on cover by Jean Arp.*

300 Marussi, Garibaldo. Determinante l'influenza di Arp sugli orientamenti della scultura. La fiera letteraria, Venice, 10. 17. 1954, p. 7.

301 Maywald. Artistes chez eux, vus par Maywald. L'architecture aujourd'hui, 2e numéro hors série consacré aux arts plastiques, Paris, 1949.

302 Meyer-Benteli, H. Konkrete Kunst. Werk 31, fasc. 4, Winterthur, April 1944.

303 Mieg, Peter. Ausstellung Jean Arp und Camille Bryen. Basler Nachrichten, 11. 30–12. 1. 1946.

304 Mili, Gjon. The Old Men of Modern Art. Life, New York, 1949. *Photo portrait.*

305 Minassian, Leone. Jean Arp. La fiera letteraria, Venice, 4. 6. 1952.

306 Moeschlin, Walter J. Hans Arp. Der Plan 2, No. 4, Vienna, 1947, p. 290.

307 Morris, George L. K. Hans Arp. Partisan Review, 4, No. 2, New York, January 1927, p. 32.

308 Mostra del Naviglio. Jean Arp. Milano, 5. 18–6. 10. 1957. *Catalogue of exhibition. Preface by Gualtieri Di San Lazzaro. Essay by Will Grohmann. Biographical and bibliographical notes.*

309 Neitzel, L. H. Hans Arp – Sophie Taeuber-Arp. Erinnerungen eines Freundes. Das Kunstwerk 2, No. 10, Baden-Baden, pp. 9–11, 39–41. *Reproductions.*

310 Netter, Maria. Arp, der glückliche Finder, der achte Beitrag unserer Umfrage "Wie sie arbeiten". Die Weltwoche, No. 1106, 1. 21. 1955.

311 Penzikis, N. G. Jean Arp. Morphes, July–August 1952, pp. 70, 71; September 1952, pp. 72, 177, 181, 216, 218. *Contains Greek translation of Arp's Jalons.*

312 Platschek, Hans. Dichtung moderner Maler. Limes-Verlag, Wiesbaden, 1956. *4 poems, 3 woodcuts by Arp. Short bibliography.*

313 Ribemont-Dessaignes, Georges. Dada painting or the oil-eye. The Little Review 9, No. 4, New York, Fall and Winter 1923/1924.

314 Richter, Hans. (On Arp.) G (periodical), Berlin, June 1924, pp. 48, 49.

315 Ritchie, Andrew Carnduff. Sculpture of the Twentieth Century. The Museum of Modern Art, New York, n. d., p. 24. *3 reproductions.*

316 Schaeffer, Cornelia. Cosmic Shape, Sculpture viewed in Art Display. European Traveller, Paris, 11. 23. 1950.

317 Schenk, Walter. Hans Arp, der Maler, Dichter und Bildhauer. Essence, Monatsschrift für Originalgraphik und Dichtung, Zurich, July–August 1951, p. 2. *Cf. No. 130.*

318 Schiess, Hans. Hans Arp. Abstraction-Creation, Art Non-Figuratif, No. 1, Paris, 1932, pp. 2, 3. *2 reproductions. Other reproductions in Nos. 2 and 3.*

319 Schneider, Camille. Jean Arp. Alsace et Moselle, Magazin Ringier, Nr. 10. Zofingen and Saint Louis, March 1951.

320 Schwitters, Kurt. An Arp. Merz 4, Hannover, Merz-Verlag, July 1923, p. 1.

321 Seuphor, Michel. Défense et illustration de l'art abstrait. In: L'Art abstrait, ses origines, ses premiers maîtres, ed. by Michel Seuphor. Maeght, Paris, 1949, pp. 62–64. *Cf. No. 120.*

322 Seuphor, Michel. Sophie Taeuber-Arp, Jean Arp. Art d'aujourd'hui, No. 10/11, Paris, 1950.

323 Seuphor, Michel. Mission spirituelle de l'Art, à propos de l'Oeuvre de Sophie Taeuber-Arp et de Jean Arp. Edition Berggruen & Cie., Paris, 1953. *Make-up and cover with the collaboration of Arp. Edition of 500 copies, of which 250 are numbered, signed, and contain a silk print.*

324 Seuphor, Michel. Dictionnaire de la Peinture Abstraite. Editions Fernand Hazan, Paris, 1957, pp. 122, 123. *Dust cover by Arp.*

325 Seuphor, Michel. Arcadie d'Arp. 74 pp. Prisme-Collection 4, ed. by Hans Hofer, Paris, 1957. *French text and English translation. Text by Will Grohmann: Hans Arp, Maler, Plastiker und Poet. Biographical and bibliographical notes by Hans Bolliger. 47 reproductions, photo portrait.*

326 Seuphor, Michel. Jean Arp. L'Oeil, No. 28, Paris and Lausanne, 1957, pp. 42–49. *18 reproductions.*

327 Soby, James Thrall. After Picasso. Dodd Mead, New York, 1935, pp. 90, 91.

328 Soergel, Albert. Dichtung und Dichter der Zeit, No. 2, R. Voigtländers Verlag, Leipzig, 1925, pp. 623, 634.

329 Spiller, Jürg. Hans Arp. Abstrakt und Konkret, No. 9/10, Zurich, 1945, p. 13–18.

330 Stahly, François. Pariser Kunstchronik, Hans Arp, Galerie Maeght. Werk 38, fasc. 1, January 1951.

331 Stedelijk Museum. 13 Beeldhouwers uit Parijs. Catalogue No. 50, Amsterdam, n. d.

332 Tériade, E. Documentation sur la jeune peinture, IV, La réaction littéraire. Cahiers d'Art 5, No. 2, Paris, 1930, pp. 72, 74, 80. *Reproductions.*

333 (Arp, Hans. Nothing at all.) Time-Magazine, New York, 1. 31. 1949, pp. 37, 38. *Interview with Arp.*

334 Torres-Garcia, Joaquin. Hans Arp, Universalismo constructivo. Editorial Poseidon, Buenos Aires, 1944, pp. 538–541.

335 Trier, Eduard. Moderne Plastik von Auguste Rodin bis Marino Marini. Büchergilde Gutenberg, Frankfurt, 1955, p. 62 f. *2 reproductions.*

336 Tzara, Tristan. Note 2 sur l'art, H. Arp. Dada 2, Zurich, December 1917, p. 2. *Contains poem dedicated to Arp: Printemps.*

337 Tzara, Tristan. Les poésies d'Arp. In: Anthologie Dada (Dada 4/5), Zurich, 5. 15. 1919. *Cf. No. 47.*

338 Tzara, Tristan. (Monsieur Aa l'antiphilosophe:) Arp. Littérature 3, No. 19, Paris, May 1921, p. 9.

339 Tzara, Tristan. Arp. Merz 6 (Arp 1). Merz-Verlag, Hannover, 1923, p. 49. *Cf. No. 57.*

340 Tzara, Tristan. Arp. Les Feuilles Libres, No. 27, Paris, 1927/1928, pp. 37–40, 44–56, 56–59.

341 Tzara, Tristan. Le papier collé, ou le proverbe en peinture. Cahiers d'Art 6, No. 2, Paris, 1931, pp. 61–64.

342 Usinger, Fritz. Der Dadaismus. In: Expressionismus, Gestalten einer literarischen Bewegung, ed. by Hermann Friedmann and Otto Mann. Wolfgang Rothe-Verlag, Heidelberg, 1956, pp. 341–350.

343 Valangin, Aline. Hans Arp als Dichter. Die Weltwoche, 5. 21. 1954.

344 Valangin, Aline. Arpiana. Basler Nachrichten, 5. 25. 1956.

345 Vallier, Dora. La XXVII Biennale de Venise. Cahiers d'Art 29, No. 1, October 1954, p. 112.

346 Vézelay, Paule. Jean Arp, castles of rejoicing. World Review, London, 1949. *4 reproductions, photo portrait.*

347 Vordemberge-Gildewart. Hans Arp. Kroniek van Kunst en Kultuur 9, No. 3, March 1948. *Photos by Maywald.*

348 Walter, Karl (ed.). Zwischen Rhein und Mosel, Elsässische und lothringische Dichtung der Gegenwart. Heitz-Verlag, Strassburg, 1933, pp. 221–225, 302.

349 Wescher, Hertha. Zeitgenössische Kunst in Paris. Nationalzeitung, Basel, 4. 19. 1952.

350 Wescher, Hertha. Pariser Kunstausstellungen, II. Nationalzeitung, Basel, 1. 22. 1956. *On Arp's collages.*

351 Wescher, Hertha. Arp. Cimaise 3, Nr. 4, Paris, March 1956. *On Arp's collages.*

352 Wescher, Hertha. Le Cosmos de Arp. Cimaise 4, No. 4, Paris, March-April 1957. *12 reproductions, photo portrait.*

353 Wilenski, Reginald Howard. Modern French painters. Reynal & Hitchcock, New York, 1940, pp. 261, 263, 267, 294.

354 Zervos, Christian. Arp (Galerie Maeght). Cahiers d'Art 25, II–1950, pp. 391–398.

Poems Set to Music

355 Blacher, Boris. Träume vom Tod und vom Leben, Kantate nach einer Dichtung von Hans Arp. Bote & Bock, Berlin, 1955. *Opus 49, for tenor solo, chorus and orchestra.*

356 Vogel, Wladimir. Arpiade, Gedichte von Hans Arp: Sekundenzeiger. Rosen schreiten. Der gordische Schlüssel. Halb Reh, halb Mädchen. Le Siège de l'air. Joie noire. Vert comme la mousse. Dernière page. Ars Viva-Verlag, 1954.